PLAY THESE HANDS WITH ME

by Terence Reese

**Published by
Devyn Press
Louisville, Kentucky**

Cover by Bonnie Baron Pollack

Devyn Press
151 Thierman Lane
Louisville, KY 40207

ISBN 0-910791-11-2

Contents

Foreword

"How do you know it's a squeeze hand, or an elimination, or whatever?" asks the player who has read about these plays but seldom brings them off at the table.

It is, indeed, one thing to understand a play in theory, another to put it into effect. In this book I seek to close the gap by describing what goes through the mind of a good player from the moment the dummy goes down until the end of the play. None of the hands is of the familiar problem type to which an answer can be formulated at trick one; in every case deductions are drawn and the picture unfolds gradually.

The formalised style, with the use of the continuous present, which I adopted in my earlier book, *Play Bridge With Reese*, and again here, has given rise to many Witty Parodies over the years. That one can bear, but I do weary of the type of criticism that goes, "Your problem (*sic*) is wrong because if the West hand had been something else and he had played in such and such a fashion, the declarer would not have made the contract in the way you describe."

Plain inaccuracies and misstatements are another matter. I have been extremely fortunate to have as long-stop Patrick Jourdain, most meticulous of players and analysts, who has saved me from numerous small errors and, I hope, all major ones.

TERENCE REESE

1. When They Die Early

One aspect of declarer's play is seldom commented upon: this is that most part-score hands can be played more accurately than most game hands. When the bidding goes one spade—four spades, very little is known about the defending hands, and even when a high contract is reached after a competitive auction there are extensions either way: one defender may have been sacrificing, the other may be hoping to defeat the final contract, one cannot always tell.

But when the contract is at the level of two or three, certain conclusions can be drawn even though both opponents may have passed throughout. For example, if you and your partner buy the contract with a combined 20 points or less, you may be sure that the outstanding strength is equally divided and also that the suits will break evenly. In a pairs you can take risks without fear of an unexpected ruff.

Clearest of all are those hands where both opponents enter the bidding and drop out at a low level. The whole picture may then be clear after a trick or two.

Playing in a pairs event against opponents who are reasonably sound bidders, I hold in second position:

♠ — ♡ 9 6 ♢ 10 8 6 5 2 ♣ A K J 10 8 7

Neither side is vulnerable and East, on my right, opens **one heart**. As the clubs are so much better than the diamonds, I prefer **two clubs** at this point to an unusual two notrumps. Depending on how the bidding develops, I may be able to bid notrumps later, to show that I can contest in either minor. Not so on this occasion, for West bids **two diamonds**. My partner joins in with **two spades**, which East **doubles**. I retreat to **three clubs**, which is passed out. The bidding has been brief but informative:

South	West	North	East
—	—	—	1♡
2♣	2♢	2♠	double
3♣	pass	pass	pass

West leads the king of diamonds and dummy is seen to have the best hand at the table:

♠ K J 9 5 2
♡ A Q J 7 5
◇ A
♣ 4 3

◇ K led

♠ —
♡ 9 6
◇ 10 8 6 5 2
♣ A K J 10 8 7

The ace of diamonds wins the first trick, East playing the 7. If the diamonds are not worse than 5 – 2 I can ruff one round. Let's consider the likely distribution.

East opened one heart and doubled two spades. West would surely have led a singleton of his partner's suit, so the hearts are probably 6 – 0. East must be credited with A Q of spades, king of hearts, and probably queen of clubs, for his opening bid; that leaves only the diamond honours for West, and he must have six for his free bid of two diamonds. As players with five spades and six hearts usually open one spade unless strong enough to reverse, East's likely shape is 4 – 6 – 1 – 2.

Plainly it would be a mistake to ruff a diamond, setting up a crossruff for the defence. I begin instead with a finesse of the jack of clubs, followed by the ace and king. East, as expected, has Q x and discards a heart on the third round.

I think now that West is out of the game and that I can take on East alone. I lead the 6 of hearts, West discards a spade, and the queen is taken by the king. This is the position now, with East on lead:

♠ K J 9 5
♡ A J 7 5
◇ —
♣ —

♠ —
♡ 9
◇ 10 8 6 5
♣ 10 8 7

East, looking unhappy, returns a low heart. Avoiding this small trap, I overtake the 9 with the jack and return the 7. East covers with the 8 and I let this hold. Now East cannot avoid giving me a tenth trick, whether he lays down the ace of spades (which will be allowed to win) or returns a heart into the A 5. The full hand was:

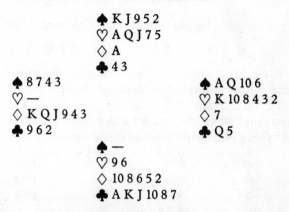

Making ten tricks in clubs produced only an average score, as it happened. Owing to the fortunate lie of the diamonds and clubs, declarers in notrumps could not help making nine tricks; a small triumph for players who overcalled with the unusual two notrumps and were left to play in that contract.

Post-mortem

Once declarer had avoided the pitfall of trying to ruff a diamond, the play of this hand was simple enough; but it is interesting to note that after the first trick it was possible to form an exact picture both of the distribution and of the division of the high cards.

2. Overtaking the Field

Playing in one of the big pairs events on the Continent, I hold as dealer:

♠ K Q 9   ♡ A J 5 3   ◇ J 4   ♣ A Q 6 2

Too strong in our system for a non-vulnerable notrump, I open **one club** and partner responds **one diamond**. When a hand fits into the range of a two notrump rebid, as this one does at Acol, I prefer to bid **two notrumps** rather than proceed with a scientific one heart. Partner raises to **three notrumps,** concluding the auction:

South	West	North	East
1♣	pass	1◇	pass
2NT	pass	3NT	pass
pass	pass		

West leads the 3 of spades and when the dummy goes down I see that it wasn't so clever to by-pass the heart suit.

```
              ♠ 6 5 2
              ♡ K 9 6 2
              ◇ A 8 5 2
              ♣ K 7
♠ 3 led
              ♠ K Q 9
              ♡ A J 5 3
              ◇ J 4
              ♣ A Q 6 2
```

East plays the ace of spades on the opening lead and returns the 10. The trouble here is that the Continentals, who almost all play a strong notrump throughout, will wheel out the old Stayman and play in four hearts, making eleven tricks if the heart finesse is right, ten if it is wrong. Playing in notrumps, I shall always be a trick behind them.

There must be a case, therefore, for a bold stroke to restore the situation. Playing against the odds, I lead the jack of hearts at trick three, intending to run it if not covered. This backward finesse will gain by force if East holds 10 x, and there is the further chance that

West may not cover with Q x, as from his angle declarer may be leading from A J 10 or A J 10 x. The jack of hearts wins in practice, and I end up with ten tricks, the full hand being:

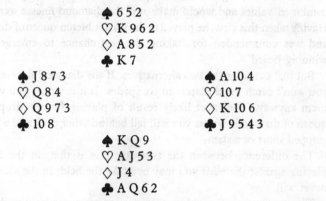

```
                ♠ 6 5 2
                ♡ K 9 6 2
                ◇ A 8 5 2
                ♣ K 7
♠ J 8 7 3                    ♠ A 10 4
♡ Q 8 4                      ♡ 10 7
◇ Q 9 7 3                    ◇ K 10 6
♣ 10 8                       ♣ J 9 5 4 3
                ♠ K Q 9
                ♡ A J 5 3
                ◇ J 4
                ♣ A Q 6 2
```

Four notrumps was a better than average score, as players in hearts generally lost a spade, a diamond and a heart.

Post-mortem

There was not very much in the play of this hand, but it will serve as a peg on which to hang a discussion about an important branch of duplicate tactics. The question is: In what circumstances is it advisable to play against the odds because you are comparing with other tables?

There is a great deal of muddled thinking in this area. Players are often exhorted to play for the drop of a singleton king or to take an abnormal finesse on the grounds that, if the cards lie normally, they are set for a bad result. But it is necessary to be clear in one's mind that if the abnormal play succeeds it will enable the declarer to overtake players in the alternative, more popular, contract. Consider this example from an eminent magazine:

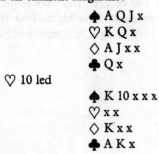

```
                ♠ A Q J x
                ♡ K Q x
                ◇ A J x x
                ♣ Q x

♡ 10 led
                ♠ K 10 x x x
                ♡ x x
                ◇ K x x
                ♣ A K x
```

South played in four spades. A heart was led to the queen and ace, and a club was returned.

The declarer judged that most pairs would bid to six spades on the combined values and would make it if the diamond finesse were right. Having taken this view, he played to drop a doubleton queen of diamonds and was commended for 'taking the best chance to emerge with a winning board'.

But just consider the two alternatives. If the diamond finesse is right you won't catch the declarers in six spades. If it is wrong you will beat them anyway. The most likely result of playing for the drop of the queen of diamonds is that you will fall behind other declarers who have stopped short of a slam.

The difference between the two examples is that, in the first, by playing against the odds you may overtake the field, in the second you never will.

The same sort of problem often arises after competitive bidding. Suppose you sacrifice in five diamonds doubled over four spades, with neither side vulnerable. Your trump holding is A x opposite K Q 10 x x x. You must be one down in any case and you realise that if trumps are 3 – 2 you could have defeated four spades. Is it sensible to play for trumps to be 4 – 1, on the grounds that this is your only chance to make a good score?

The answer is that the die is already cast. If diamonds are 3 – 2 you have made a phantom sacrifice and whether you go one or two down won't matter in relation to pairs who have defeated four spades. If diamonds are 4 – 1 you have made a good sacrifice and will beat all the pairs who allowed their opponents to play four spades.

The pairs you have to consider are not those who defend against four spades but those who, like yourself, play in diamonds or defend against a part score in spades. If you can keep the loss to 100 you will beat pairs who may have lost 140 or 170. You may judge (from the confidence with which your opponents have bid to four spades) that the diamonds are 4 – 1, and it may be right to finesse for that reason— but only for that reason.

3. Undercover Work

It tends to be a mistake, I have noticed, when you know your partner
has made a psychic bid, to double the final contract. It is better to let
the declarer misplace the lie of the cards. What would have happened
on the following deal if East had not doubled is hard to say.

In a mixed game of rubber bridge, with neither side vulnerable, I
hold in second position:

♠ 7 ♡ 10 8 6 3 ◇ A J 8 4 ♣ Q 9 6 2

After two passes the opponent on my left opens **one heart,** my
partner doubles, and the next hand passes. One notrump is a possibility
now (partner must hold the spades), and in a pairs I might bid that.
However, there might be a good contract in one of the minors, so I
bid a straightforward **two diamonds.** Partner bids **two hearts,** their
suit. I take that as a forward-going move and show my second suit,
three clubs. Partner puts on speed with **four notrumps.** I respond
dutifully **five diamonds** and he advances to **six diamonds.** No one is
surprised when East **doubles.** That concludes the auction:

South	West	North	East
—	—	—	pass
pass	1♡	double	pass
2◇	pass	2♡	pass
3♣	pass	4NT	pass
5◇	pass	6◇	double
pass	pass	pass	

West leads the 10 of spades and I am not overjoyed to see this dummy:

♠ A K J 4
♡ A 9
◇ K 6 5 2
♣ A K 5

♠ 10 led

♠ 7
♡ 10 8 6 3
◇ A J 8 4
♣ Q 9 6 2

7

One thing is clear: West has opened a psychic one heart and East has all the strength in the other suits, including, no doubt, four good trumps.

It is no use trying to ruff hearts in dummy. I must play on reverse-dummy lines, ruffing two spades in hand. I take the ace of spades, finesse the jack of diamonds successfully, and cross to the ace of hearts, on which East drops the king. After king of spades and a spade ruff I play a club to the ace and ruff a fourth spade, to which all follow. A club to the king stands up and the king of diamonds is cashed. The situation is now more hopeful:

♠ –
♡ 9
◇ 6
♣ 5

♠ –
♡ 10
◇ –
♣ Q 9

I thought at the beginning that I would need to win four club tricks to provide a discard for dummy's heart, but of course that's not necessary. If anyone has four clubs it will be East, and he will have to follow suit when the last round is ruffed. After queen of clubs and a club ruff East's winning trump and West's winning heart fall with a thud on the last trick. East is disconsolate, as may be gathered from a sight of the full hand:

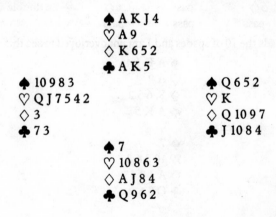

```
                    ♠ A K J 4
                    ♡ A 9
                    ◇ K 6 5 2
                    ♣ A K 5
♠ 10 9 8 3                          ♠ Q 6 5 2
♡ Q J 7 5 4 2                       ♡ K
◇ 3                                 ◇ Q 10 9 7
♣ 7 3                               ♣ J 10 8 4
                    ♠ 7
                    ♡ 10 8 6 3
                    ◇ A J 8 4
                    ♣ Q 9 6 2
```

This was the position round the table at the finish:

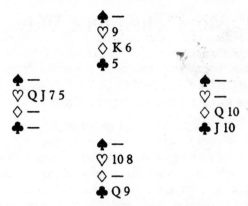

♠ —
♡ 9
◇ K 6
♣ 5

♠ —
♡ Q J 7 5
◇ —
♣ —

♠ —
♡ —
◇ Q 10
♣ J 10

♠ —
♡ 10 8
◇ —
♣ Q 9

Declarer cashed the king of diamonds, led a club to the queen, and ruffed a club, losing the last trick in two places, as it were.

The ending belongs to the same family as the *coup-en-passant*, where the declarer makes a low trump because he plays after the opponent who holds the master trump. Here the low trump is made in front of the winning one. I think of this as "undercover play" because declarer makes his losing trump under cover of the opponent's obligation to follow suit.

The play of this hand proceeded quite easily once declarer had formed the right general plan. However, some players would have gone wrong at the start. Thinking that there were certain losers in hearts and trumps, they might have taken a desperate finesse of the jack of spades at trick one, hoping to discard two hearts on the A K of spades, discard a heart from dummy on the fourth club, and ruff the last heart. Or they might have led the king of diamonds early on, hoping to find West with a singleton 9 or 10 and then to pick up the trumps without loss. This must be the wrong line because the only sensible plan is to reverse the dummy, using South's low trumps for spade ruffs.

4. More Than One Way

Playing in a pairs event, with both sides vulnerable, I hold in third position:

♠ A Q 8 3   ♡ Q 5   ◇ 10 7 5   ♣ K J 9 2

Against my better judgement I have agreed to play a weak notrump throughout, so after two passes the choice is between pass, one club, one spade, and one notrump. I would be happy to pass, but partners become unreasonably upset when after a throw-in they find that plus 90 has been recorded at other tables. (One never gets any credit for passing when there is a row of minus scores.) As one club has no defensive value, and opponents are quick to double a weak notrump opposite a passed hand, I decide in favour of **one spade**.

The next player passes and partner raises to **three spades,** where we rest.

South	West	North	East
—	—	pass	pass
1♠	pass	3♠	pass
pass	pass		

West leads the 4 of diamonds and I see that partner hasn't got much either, for his double raise.

```
                    ♠ J 9 6 4
                    ♡ A 10 8 7 3
                    ◇ J 6
                    ♣ Q 10

◇ 4 led
                    ♠ A Q 8 3
                    ♡ Q 5
                    ◇ 10 7 5
                    ♣ K J 9 2
```

I don't care for this, because players who open one club or one notrump will be able to stop in two spades.

East wins the first trick with the ace of diamonds and returns the 3. West plays the king and leads a third diamond, which dummy ruffs.

Digressing for a moment, I find that when opponents lead a suit in which, as declarer, one has no interest, it is easy not to notice what is happening. Later in the hand, when one is trying to work out who has shown what, the play to the first two or three tricks is a distant blur.

However, on this occasion it registers on me that East has A Q of diamonds and West the king. Also, the fall of the cards is consistent with a 5 – 3 break, as no-one has led the 2.

The contract of three spades appears to depend on not losing a trump trick, but in some circumstances I may be able to avoid losing a heart. I think I'll test the clubs first, to discover who has the ace. The 10 of clubs is led to the king and a club return is taken by East's ace.

That's interesting. East has turned up with A Q of diamonds and ace of clubs. The king of spades would give him 13 points and most players feel it incumbent upon them to open the bidding with that number. So the spade finesse is surely wrong.

East exits with a club, which I win with the jack. These cards are left:

```
          ♠ J 9 6
          ♡ A 10 8 7
          ◇ —
          ♣ —


          ♠ A Q 8 3
          ♡ Q 5
          ◇ —
          ♣ 9
```

I have chances to end-play West if he began with K x of spades and the king of hearts. I play off the ace of spades and then the 9 of clubs, to extract a possible fourth club from the West hand. West follows suit and I ruff with the jack of spades to avoid a possible over-ruff. The only chance now is to find West with the king of spades alone and no more diamonds. I am in luck, for West wins the next round of trumps with the king and leads a heart, which runs to my queen. I have lost only two diamonds, a club, and a trump. The full hand was:

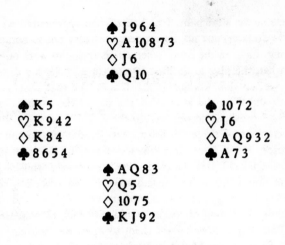

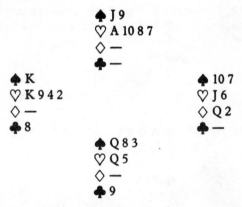

Post-mortem

This was the position round the table after the ace of spades had been played off:

Leading the 9 of clubs and ruffing with the jack of spades might have led to two down, but the risk had to be taken because even one down would have been a poor result.

The principle illustrated by this deal is: *When there is more than one way to play a suit, postpone the play, even when it is the trump suit. You may gain a useful indication.* When declarer found that East held ♢ A Q and ♣ A he could place West with the king of spades. The next step was to find him with K x alone and force a lead up to the queen of hearts.

5. Where Battles Are Won

M. Harrison Gray, the great British player of the nineteen-fifties and sixties, would always play off a long suit in preference to alternative lines of play. At the finish, he always seemed to know what was troubling an opponent and how the cards lay. Indeed, it is surprising how many inferences can be drawn on every hand, once one gives one's mind to them.

My opponents in a team-of-four match are both good players. Our side is vulnerable when as dealer I pick up:

♠ 7　♡ Q 6　◇ A Q 10 7 6 3 2　♣ A 10 5

I open **one diamond** and my partner responds **one heart**. The next player, East, comes in with **two spades**, which is described as "intermediate". I venture **three diamonds**, West bids **three spades** and my partner **four diamonds**. East passes, I have no more to offer, and West also passes, though with some reluctance. The bidding has been:

South	West	North	East
1◇	pass	1♡	2♠
3◇	3♠	4◇	pass
pass	pass		

West leads the 3 of spades and partner puts down:

♠ J 6 4
♡ A 8 5 2
◇ K J 9
♣ J 8 4

♠ 3 led

♠ 7
♡ Q 6
◇ A Q 10 7 6 3 2
♣ A 10 5

East wins the first trick with the king of spades and returns a low spade, which I ruff. I play a diamond to the jack and ruff the third spade, bringing down the queen from West. When I play a second trump to the king West discards the 3 of hearts. That leaves:

♠ —
♡ A 8 5 2
◇ 9
♣ J 8 4

♠ —
♡ Q 6
◇ A Q 7
♣ A 10 5

I have lost one trick and am in danger of losing a heart and two clubs. What do I know about the hand so far? West is marked with Q x x of spades and a singleton diamond. His heart discard suggests that he began with five, and as East did not lead a club up to the weakness at trick two the club honours are probably divided, unless East holds both.

I could lead a heart up to the queen, but if that went wrong I would have little play left. My instinct is to play trumps and see what turns up. Both defenders are going to be under pressure.

On two rounds of diamonds West discards a club and a heart, East a couple of spades. On the last diamond West throws a club and East a heart. We are down now to:

♠ —
♡ A 8 5
◇ —
♣ J 8

♠ —
♡ Q 6
◇ —
♣ A 10 5

West, I am sure, has kept three hearts to the king and two clubs. East has only one spade left, so it is safe to lead a low club. West plays low without a tremor and the jack loses to the king. East cashes his spade and exits with a heart to the queen, king and ace. At trick twelve I lead a club to the A 10. Reflecting (1) that if East had held ♣ K Q he would surely have kept two spades, and (2) that West was dubious about passing four diamonds, I go up with the ace of clubs and drop the queen. The full hand was:

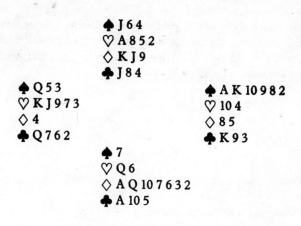

♠ J 6 4
♡ A 8 5 2
◇ K J 9
♣ J 8 4

♠ Q 5 3
♡ K J 9 7 3
◇ 4
♣ Q 7 6 2

♠ A K 10 9 8 2
♡ 10 4
◇ 8 5
♣ K 9 3

♠ 7
♡ Q 6
◇ A Q 10 7 6 3 2
♣ A 10 5

Post-mortem

This was the position when the last trump was led;

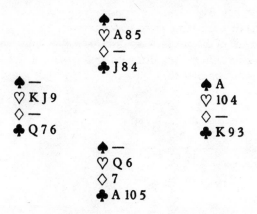

♠ —
♡ A 8 5
◇ —
♣ J 8 4

♠ —
♡ K J 9
◇ —
♣ Q 7 6

♠ A
♡ 10 4
◇ —
♣ K 9 3

♠ —
♡ Q 6
◇ 7
♣ A 10 5

West had to let go a club on the last trump because if he discards a heart declarer can lead the queen of hearts and duck it.

East would have done better to keep two spades and a club fewer, but the spades were easy discards and he let them go too early.

The interest of the hand lies in the number of inferences that the declarer was able to draw. It may seem a lot to think about, but many of them (for example that West, discarding a heart in front of dummy, must hold five) occur frequently and should be automatic.

The declarer took a risk of a sort when he abandoned the legitimate chance of finding East with the king of hearts in favour of a pressure

15

play to which there would probably be a defence. Players tend to go for the legitimate chance on these occasions, because if it fails they will have a sound defence in the post-mortem; but that is not where battles are won.

6. The Cross-breed

Playing rubber bridge with a partner of somewhat unpredictable habits, I hold in third position:

♠ K 10 9 6 4   ♡ A 8   ◇ 8 6 4 3   ♣ A J

With neither side vulnerable, my partner deals and opens **one heart.** I respond **one spade** and partner rebids **one notrump.** As we are playing a strong notrump throughout, I take this to be a limited hand in the 12 – 14 range. At this point the player on my right intervenes with **two clubs.**

I was intending to raise one notrump to three notrumps, but with no certainty of making it. The intervention seems to present our side with a likely 300 and a chance of 500. Doubles with short trumps often work out well because the declarer misplaces the cards. Taking this view, I **double** two clubs.

Partner removes the double to **two spades.** Well, I am not going to hang in a part score with 12 points opposite an opening bid, so I go to **four spades,** which is passed out. The bidding has been:

South	West	North	East
—	—	1♡	pass
1♠	pass	1NT	2♣
double	pass	2♠	pass
4♠	pass	pass	pass

West leads the 7 of clubs and partner puts down this moderate collection:

♠ A Q J
♡ 10 7 4 3
◇ K 10 9
♣ Q 8 4

♣ 7 led

♠ K 10 9 6 4
♡ A 8
◇ 8 6 4 3
♣ A J

To open a major suit on 10 7 4 3 gives me the shudders, and I would rather be defending against two clubs doubled than trying to make four spades.

There are only eight tricks on top and clearly I must try to develop a trick or two in diamonds. As I may want to negotiate a ruff of the fourth diamond, it must be right to tackle this suit before drawing trumps.

The club lead runs to my jack and I lead a diamond. When West plays low I finesse the 9, losing to the queen. East cashes the ace of diamonds, then plays a club, which I take with the ace, West following suit.

East looks a little disgruntled. No doubt, he has A Q of diamonds alone and expected his partner to ruff the second club (remember, I doubled two clubs) and give him a diamond ruff.

I may still be able to ruff the fourth diamond, as planned. If East has only two trumps I can draw two rounds, cash the king of diamonds, return to the ace of hearts, and ruff a diamond.

But when I play off ace and queen of spades, West shows out. These cards are left:

♠ J
♡ 10 7 4 3
♢ K
♣ Q

♠ K 10 9
♡ A 8
♢ 8 6
♣ —

It's no use trying to cash the king of diamonds now, because East will ruff it. The heart is a certain loser. What can I do about the fourth diamond?

Let me see. East is presumably 4 – 1 – 2 – 6. So West has control of both hearts and diamonds.

Three more discards will surely embarrass him. I cash the jack of spades, ruff the queen of clubs to confirm the count of that suit, and play off my last spade. West has discarded three hearts, perforce. Now I play ace and another heart and dummy's 10 of hearts is a winner. The full hand was:

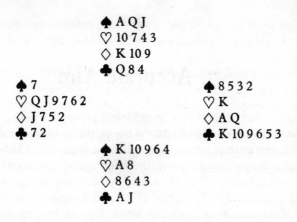

```
              ♠ A Q J
              ♡ 10 7 4 3
              ◇ K 10 9
              ♣ Q 8 4
♠ 7                          ♠ 8 5 3 2
♡ Q J 9 7 6 2                ♡ K
◇ J 7 5 2                    ◇ A Q
♣ 7 2                        ♣ K 10 9 6 5 3
              ♠ K 10 9 6 4
              ♡ A 8
              ◇ 8 6 4 3
              ♣ A J
```

Post-mortem

As the defence went, this was not a difficult hand to play. It stayed in my mind because the "criss-cross squeeze without the count" is quite a rarity. This was the position when the last trump was led:

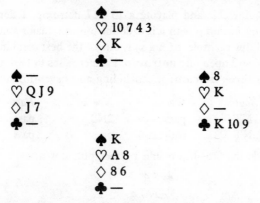

```
              ♠ —
              ♡ 10 7 4 3
              ◇ K
              ♣ —
♠ —                          ♠ 8
♡ Q J 9                      ♡ K
◇ J 7                        ◇ —
♣ —                          ♣ K 10 9
              ♠ K
              ♡ A 8
              ◇ 8 6
              ♣ —
```

If the king of hearts had been played earlier and been ducked by the declarer, there would have been a standard criss-cross squeeze, South holding at the finish ♡ A and ◇ 8 6 opposite ♡ 10 7 and ◇ K. The unusual feature in the diagram above was that a trick had to be lost after the squeeze card had been played.

7. Accurate Aim

Sometimes an early lead by a defender will present the declarer with an awkward choice: should he take the finesse that is offered or should he spurn it and attempt to run for home in the other suits? Nobody likes to take a finesse and go down, then find that the contract was cold without the finesse. Thus there may be some psychological pressure to win the critical trick. On the whole, it is a pressure that should be resisted. If the finesse loses, the worst may not happen, for various reasons; and the more that declarer is able to learn about the hand, the more accurate his aim is likely to be at the finish.

Playing rubber bridge against experienced opponents, I hold as dealer:

♠ A J 10 5   ♡ Q 8   ◇ A K 4   ♣ K 8 7 2

We are vulnerable and playing a 15 – 17 notrump. I don't like to open a strong notrump with a low doubleton in a major suit, but Q x (as opposed, for example, to A x x) is one of the best combinations for the declarer, so I open **one notrump**. Partner raises to **two notrumps** and I go to **three notrumps**, concluding an uneventful auction:

South	West	North	East
1NT	pass	2NT	pass
3NT	pass	pass	pass

West leads the 5 of hearts and partner puts down:

♠ 7 4
♡ K 7 3
◇ J 10 8 2
♣ A J 5 3

♡ 5 led

♠ A J 10 5
♡ Q 8
◇ A K 4
♣ K 8 7 2

Although we have 26 points and fair intermediates, the hands do not fit too well and it's going to be a borderline affair.

I play low from dummy on the heart lead, East plays the 10 and I win with the queen. It is natural to play on clubs first, taking the finesse towards East. I lead the king of clubs and follow with the 8, keeping the entries fluid. The jack loses to the queen and East returns the 9 of spades.

This is the type of situation mentioned in the preamble above. The risk of putting in the 10 of spades is that the defenders may defeat the contract at once by taking three heart tricks, while I have chances to make nine tricks by way of one spade, one heart, four diamonds, and three clubs. However, the hand may develop in a number of ways and I don't want to commit myself to one line of play. Assuming that West's lead of the 5 of hearts was fourth best, the defence can take three heart tricks only if the lead was from J 9 6 5 precisely. Trusting that the hearts will not be so hostile, I put in the 10 of spades, which loses to the queen. West now leads the jack of hearts.

Yes, I expected that. He may, of course, be underleading the ace, but in these situations it is usually safe to assume that East's reason for not returning his partner's suit when in with the queen of clubs was that he held the ace of hearts over dummy's king. The choice of the 9 of spades, rather than a low one, is a further indication that East expects his partner to return a heart rather than develop tricks in spades. I play low from dummy, therefore. East wins the next trick with the ace of hearts and leads the 8 of spades. I have lost four tricks and the position is:

♠ 7
♡ —
♢ J 10 8 2
♣ A 5

♠ A J
♡ —
♢ A K 4
♣ 7 2

The spade finesse by itself won't give me nine tricks and I don't fancy it anyway—not so much because East led the 9 followed by the 8 as because West gave no thought to returning the suit after the jack of hearts had held. I go up with the ace of spades, therefore, play off the ace of diamonds, then lead the 7 of clubs to dummy's ace, East discarding a spade. Now we are down to:

♠ —
♡ —
◇ J 10 8
♣ 5

♠ J
♡ —
◇ K 4
♣ 2

I could play East for Q x x of diamonds, but let's do some counting. West is known to have begun with five hearts and three clubs and, I think, still has the king of spades. If that's right, he has only a doubleton diamond and the finesse won't help me. So I play the 8 of diamonds to the king and am happy to see the queen drop, the full hand being:

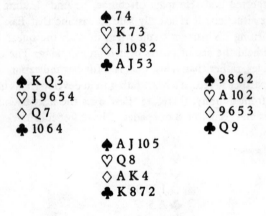

♠ 7 4
♡ K 7 3
◇ J 10 8 2
♣ A J 5 3

♠ K Q 3
♡ J 9 6 5 4
◇ Q 7
♣ 10 6 4

♠ 9 8 6 2
♡ A 10 2
◇ 9 6 5 3
♣ Q 9

♠ A J 10 5
♡ Q 8
◇ A K 4
♣ K 8 7 2

Post-mortem

Despite its ordinary appearance, this hand contained a number of interesting features:

The unblock of the 8 and 7 of clubs—routine, of course, and, as it happened, not needed at the finish.

The decision to play the 10 of spades at trick 4, not the ace. This would have been a mistake, it is true, if West had held J 9 6 5 of hearts and East Q x x of diamonds; but by developing the hand slowly declarer learned more about the distribution.

The decision to duck the second round of hearts. This was based on the inference that if East had not held the ace he would have returned the suit.

The count of West's hand at the finish, which showed that the only chance to make four tricks in diamonds was to drop the queen.

8. Through the Slips

In a pairs event, with neither side vulnerable, I hold as dealer:

♠ Q 10 3   ♡ A   ◇ A K J 9 6 4   ♣ A K 7

Playing Acol, I open **two diamonds,** forcing for one round. Partner raises to **three diamonds.** The direct raise guarantees an ace, so there must be slam chances. We normally show the lowest control, so I proceed with **three hearts.** He raises to **four hearts,** which is not very helpful; perhaps my three hearts wasn't a good choice. As he has declined to show the ace of spades, which I know he must hold, he must be minimum. However, there are probably ten tricks on top in notrumps, so it is no use languishing in five diamonds. I am committed to **six diamonds,** which is passed out. The bidding has been:

South	West	North	East
2◇	pass	3◇	pass
3♡	pass	4♡	pass
6◇	pass	pass	pass

West leads the 3 of clubs and the dummy is not encouraging:

♠ A 6
♡ 9 6 4 3
◇ Q 8 5
♣ 10 8 4 2

♣ 3 led

♠ Q 10 3
♡ A
◇ A K J 9 6 4
♣ A K 7

East plays the queen of clubs and I win with the ace. On the surface, there are certain losers in spades and clubs. With only ten tricks on top, I don't see much chance of end-playing West, even if he has control of both black suits.

Prospects of making the contract by any legitimate play are so slight that I am going to try a deceptive move. Suppose I return a low club at once: if West began with J 9 x x there is a good chance that he will place his partner with K Q x and play low to prevent me from establishing a trick with ♣ 10.

I return the 7 of clubs, therefore, and with scarcely a thought West plays low. I go up with the 10 of clubs and it holds the trick. Well, that's one hurdle surmounted, but I still have to manage the spades. After a round of trumps the position is:

♠ A 6
♡ 9 6 4 3
◇ Q 8
♣ 8 4

♠ Q 10 3
♡ A
◇ K J 9 6 4
♣ K

A 2 – 2 trump break would see me home, but I don't want to give the defence a chance to draw a third round. My idea is to lead the queen of spades from hand. If this loses to East there will be no danger of a club ruff. If the queen is covered by the king I can cash the queen of diamonds and return a spade to the 10 3, making the contract if East has either king or jack of spades. So in the diagram position I lead ♠ Q.

West, who has been looking gloomy since the second trick, covers the queen, though in a manner that makes it clear to me that he does not hold K J. I can afford to play off the queen of diamonds now, because it won't bother me if East is able to win the next spade with the jack and play a third trump. East follows to ◇ Q and West discards a heart.

When I lead a spade from dummy East goes into a small trance. Finally he plays low, obviously hoping that his partner will be able to win the trick and give him a ruff in clubs. Instead, my 10 wins, the last spade is ruffed, and I end up with an overtrick, the full hand being:

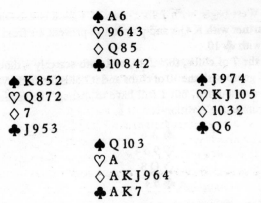

```
              ♠ A 6
              ♡ 9 6 4 3
              ◇ Q 8 5
              ♣ 10 8 4 2
♠ K 8 5 2                    ♠ J 9 7 4
♡ Q 8 7 2                    ♡ K J 10 5
◇ 7                         ◇ 10 3 2
♣ J 9 5 3                    ♣ Q 6
              ♠ Q 10 3
              ♡ A
              ◇ A K J 9 6 4
              ♣ A K 7
```

East led the assault. "What happened to the jack of clubs?" he demanded.

"The same as happened to the jack of spades," snapped West. "We didn't make it."

Post-mortem

There were some instructive plays in this deal—the immediate return of the low club, the avoidance play in spades, the timing of the trump leads.

The deceptive play at trick two can be tried with other combinations, and it is well to be prepared.

(1)

```
              10 8 5 2
Q 9 7 3                  K 4
              A J 6
```

On the first trick South heads the king with the ace. If he immediately returns the 6, West will place his partner with K J x. Having won this trick with the 10, declarer may later be able to discard the losers in one hand or the other.

(2)

```
              J 9 5 3
Q 7 6 4                 10 2
              A K 8
```

Declarer plays low from dummy on the opening lead and heads the 10 with the ace. A prompt return of the 8 will almost surely win the trick.

9. Enterprising, But Unlucky

"I have heard you say," a friend remarked to me, "that at rubber bridge you like a partner who has a bit of push and enterprise."

"Yes, indeed."

"What would you say of a partner who, over an opposing two clubs, bid an immediate grand slam?"

"Most commendable."

"Yes; but it didn't do us much good in the end. Suppose you had been South. Your hand is:

♠ A K Q 10 8 6 5 ♡ — ◇ A K J 7 ♣ A 5

Vulnerable against not, you open **two clubs** and the player on your left (he mentioned an eccentric player of my acquaintance) overcalls with **seven hearts.** When this comes round to you, you bid **seven spades,** I suppose?"

"Yes."

"Right. You've got the bidding?"

South	West	North	East
2♣	7♡	pass	pass
7♠	pass	pass	pass

"West leads the king of hearts and this is what you see:

```
              ♠ 7 4 2
              ♡ 10 6 4
              ◇ 6 5 3
              ♣ K 8 4 2

♡ K led

              ♠ A K Q 10 8 6 5
              ♡ —
              ◇ A K J 7
              ♣ A 5
```

"East plays the 3 of hearts. You ruff and play the ace of spades, **on** which West discards a heart. How would you play it?"

I gave the matter some thought. Unless he plays to drop the queen of diamonds, declarer will have to take a diamond finesse eventually. So it all turns on what he can do about the fourth diamond, assuming they are not 3 – 3.

The obvious line is to take two rounds of trumps, cash ace of diamonds, cross to king of clubs and finesse the jack of diamonds. If East holds ◇ Q x x x or more, which is not unlikely, you can ruff the fourth round.

The alternative is to play off all the trumps, playing for a real or imaginary squeeze. If East began with four diamonds and five clubs he could be squeezed. But in that case the other play—ruffing the fourth diamond—would also work.

Is there any other squeeze possibility? Yes, if West held 10 x x x of diamonds and all the top hearts he could be squeezed in the red suits. But it must be against the odds for a player who probably has eight or nine hearts to hold length in another suit.

"I'm a simple player," I said eventually. "I would finesse the jack of diamonds and play to ruff the fourth diamond if necessary."

"You wouldn't have made it. This declarer just played off all the trumps. I'll show you the full hand, you will see what happened."

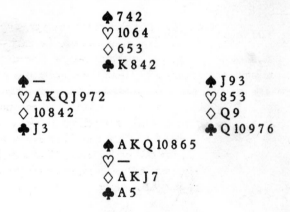

The end position was the one I had foreseen but had rejected as unlikely:

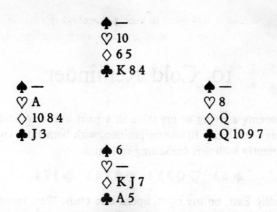

```
                    ♠ —
                    ♡ 10
                    ◇ 6 5
                    ♣ K 8 4
    ♠ —                         ♠ —
    ♡ A                         ♡ 8
    ◇ 10 8 4                    ◇ Q
    ♣ J 3                       ♣ Q 10 9 7
                    ♠ 6
                    ♡ —
                    ◇ K J 7
                    ♣ A 5
```

West must throw a club on the last spade and when South continues with ace and king of clubs he cannot spare either a heart or a diamond.

Post-mortem

I reckon that West, after his spectacular advance sacrifice, was a little unlucky to run into a hand where the opponent was able to gamble a grand slam on his own.

If there is a moral to the play, it is that, when there are alternative possibilities, very often the best plan is to lead out the long suit and hope. (Compare hand no. 5.) It may be extremely difficult for the opponents to find the right discards. Here the squeeze was genuine, but many such contracts are made because of imperfect discarding.

There was an interesting point in the bidding, not mentioned in the narrative above. As South, what, if anything, would you make of partner's pass over seven hearts? I think that, in an expert partnership, this should suggest one or two useful cards. With a really bad hand North should double, to deter his partner from any flight of fancy such as seven spades in the present instance.

10. Cold Reminder

The opponents arriving at my table in a pairs event are still arguing about a previous hand. In second position, with both sides vulnerable, I wait patiently with this unexciting collection:

♠ 6 3   ♡ Q 9 6 4   ◇ 8 7 4 2   ♣ J 7 4

Eventually East, on my right, opens **one club,** West responds **one diamond,** and my partner **doubles.** East bids **two clubs** and this is passed round to North, who **doubles** again. I respond with a dutiful **two hearts** and my partner raises this to **three hearts.**

This is very strong bidding on his part, because I might have been forced to bid two hearts on a three-card suit. My partner, who is a very good player, will have had that in mind. At the risk of being accused of making a master bid (not a complimentary term in bridge parlance), I am going to **four hearts.** East gives this contract a wistful look, but nobody doubles. The bidding has been:

South	West	North	East
—	—	—	1♣
pass	1◇	double	2♣
pass	pass	double	pass
2♡	pass	3♡	pass
4♡	pass	pass	pass

West leads the 3 of clubs and my partner's hand is about what I expected:

> ♠ A Q 10 7
> ♡ K J 10 8 5
> ◇ A Q 5
> ♣ 6

♣ 3 led

> ♠ 6 3
> ♡ Q 9 6 4
> ◇ 8 7 4 2
> ♣ J 7 4

East wins the first trick with the king of clubs and switches to the 3 of diamonds. West puts in the 9 and dummy's queen wins.

At this stage it looks like a loser in each suit, as I am not hopeful about the spade finesse. However, East's diamond was no doubt a singleton, and if I can slip through a round of trumps I may be able to put him on play later.

At trick three I lead the jack of hearts from dummy, hoping that I will look like a man who is locked on the table and has nothing else to play. East studies this card for a moment, then plays low, and I overtake with the queen.

I must think for a moment about the spade situation. West appears to have K J 10 9 x of diamonds and probably Q x x of clubs. With the king of spades as well he would have bid three clubs at some point. The king of spades is surely wrong and a finesse of the 10 won't help me much, even if it forces the king. With a different plan in mind, I ruff a club, on which West plays the 8, and lead another trump. East wins and West follows suit.

East now leads the ace of clubs, felling his partner's queen. Instead of ruffing, I discard a diamond from the table.

There is a long pause. Finally, West says icily to his partner, "It's your lead."

East, who had expected me to ruff the club in dummy, demands to see the last trick. After some thought he exits with a fourth club. I discard a spade and ruff on the table. We are now down to:

```
      ♠ A Q 10 7
      ♡ 10
      ◇ A
      ♣ —


      ♠ 6
      ♡ 9 6
      ◇ 8 7 2
      ♣ —
```

With only one trump in dummy for two diamond losers, I still need a second trick from spades. It's clear that East is 4 – 2 – 1 – 6, so I play ace followed by queen of spades, hoping to bring down J x x eventually. East covers the queen with the king, I ruff, and the 8 falls from West.

That creates a new possibility. If West's spades are 9 8 x I can lead the 10 from dummy on the next round and pin the 9. However, with that holding he might have dropped the 9. Also, if East had held ♠ K J x x ♡ A x ◇ x ♣ A K 10 x x x he would probably have doubled four hearts, knowing that his spade honours were over the strong hand.

Pursuing my original plan, I cross to the ace of diamonds and lead the 7 of spades. As I hoped, this brings down the jack and the 10 of spades is my tenth trick. The full hand was:

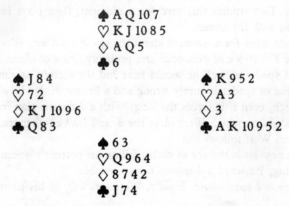

```
                    ♠ A Q 10 7
                    ♡ K J 10 8 5
                    ◇ A Q 5
                    ♣ 6
     ♠ J 8 4                      ♠ K 9 5 2
     ♡ 7 2                        ♡ A 3
     ◇ K J 10 9 6                 ◇ 3
     ♣ Q 8 3                      ♣ A K 10 9 5 2
                    ♠ 6 3
                    ♡ Q 9 6 4
                    ◇ 8 7 4 2
                    ♣ J 7 4
```

"You have become quite an enterprising bidder in your old age," observed my partner.

Post-mortem

As West pointed out with some asperity, East had two chances to defeat the contract. He could have avoided all danger of a throw-in by going up with the ace of hearts and leading another. Having failed to do that, he could still have escaped the end-play by leading a low club instead of the ace, when in with the ace of hearts. It just did not occur to him that instead of ruffing the club I might discard a diamond from dummy and leave him on play.

11. Enigmatic Reply

My opponents at rubber bridge are both experienced players, my partner not too reliable. Our side is vulnerable and in second position I hold:

♠ J 6 4　♡ A 10 9 8 6 5 3　♢ 5 2　♣ 9

East passes, and as my hearts are too weak for a vulnerable pre-empt I pass also. West opens **one notrump** (12 – 14 in principle), my partner **doubles**, and East bids **two spades**. I enter with **four hearts** and West now produces a surprising **five clubs**. My partner goes to **five hearts,** which is passed out. It has been a peculiar auction:

South	West	North	East
—	—	—	pass
pass	1NT	double	2♠
4♡	5♣	5♡	pass
pass	pass		

West leads the king of clubs and my partner puts down this moderate collection, with which he has doubled one notrump and then raised to five hearts!

```
              ♠ A 10 8
              ♡ K 7 2
              ♢ A Q 8 4
              ♣ 7 4 2

   ♣ K led
              ♠ J 6 4
              ♡ A 10 9 8 6 5 3
              ♢ 5 2
              ♣ 9
```

East plays the 5 of clubs on the first trick and West switches to the 3 of spades.

It looks natural to play low from dummy, but there are strange elements in the whole affair and before I do anything hasty I must try to work out what is happening.

To begin with, what is the spade situation? East must have at least five and West would not have led a low card from K x or Q x. He probably has six or seven clubs and not many losers in the major suits. After all, he bid five clubs very much under the gun. He might hold a doubleton 3 – 2 of spades, but if I duck this trick I don't see how I am going to avoid a second loser in spades. I *can* see chances if West's spade is a singleton. My general plan will be to let West win either the third round of clubs or the fourth round of diamonds, while I discard a spade from my own hand. Then, if my elimination has been successful, he will have to give me a ruff-and-discard.

I go up with the ace of spades, therefore, and ruff a club, on which East plays the 6. All follow to the ace of hearts. As East has not played high-low in clubs I am going to play for West to hold six clubs and four diamonds. There are just enough entries for the projected end-play. A finesse of the queen of diamonds holds and the third club is ruffed, East following with the queen. That leaves:

```
        ♠ 10 8
        ♡ K 7
        ◇ A 8 4
        ♣ —


        ♠ J 6
        ♡ 10 9 8 6
        ◇ 5
        ♣ —
```

I play a diamond to the ace and ruff a diamond. West plays the king on this trick, but he would do that anyway and I am sure he has the last diamond. Pursuing my plan, I lead a heart to the king, West following suit, then play a fourth diamond from dummy, discarding one of my spades. West wins and has to concede a ruff-and-discard, allowing me to dispose of the other spade loser. The full hand was:

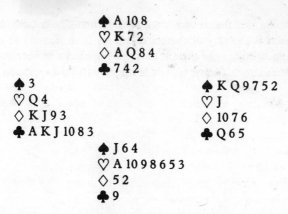

Some players would have bid the West hand differently, I dare say, but we shelter all types at my club.

I suggested to my partner that 500 from five clubs doubled would have been an easier way to make a living. "As I had nothing in clubs I knew you'd make five hearts," was the enigmatic reply.

Post-mortem

The end-game was a standard loser-on-loser ruff-and-discard elimination:

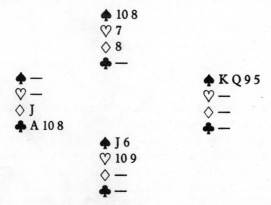

By leading a diamond from dummy and discarding a spade, South was able to transform two spade losers into one.

The main lesson of the hand is that when the bidding has been odd it is advisable to pause and review the whole sequence until a picture has been formed that is consistent with events. The critical moment of this deal was the play of the ace of spades from dummy at trick two. Although West, in the distant past, had opened one notrump, it was possible to conclude that his spade might well be a singleton.

12. Timely Discard

There are, broadly speaking, two ways of playing the "unusual notrump" overcall. Some players use it freely on weak distributional hands, others on strong two-suiters only. I support the second theory myself, believing that the weak overcalls all too often help the opponents in both bidding and play. On this hand from a team event I benefited from the knowledge that East held the same opinion. With both sides vulnerable I hold in fourth position:

♠ A K 9 8 5 4 2   ♡ 5   ◇ 8 5 4 3   ♣ J

After a pass by the dealer my partner opens **one diamond.** The next player overcalls with **two notrumps,** indicating a two-suiter composed of the lowest-ranking suits, hearts and clubs in this instance. Whether three spades would be forcing at this stage is a point not fully determined by the theorists. Anyway, I decide to bid **four spades.** West **doubles** and all pass. The bidding has been:

South	West	North	East
—	pass	1◇	2NT
4♠	double	pass	pass
pass			

West opens the 10 of hearts and partner puts down:

♠ Q
♡ K Q J
◇ K J 6 2
♣ A 8 5 4 2

♡ 10 led

♠ A K 9 8 5 4 2
♡ 5
◇ 8 5 4 3
♣ J

The diamonds are disappointing. I suppose he opened one diamond because he did not fancy the sequence, 1♣ – 1♠ – 2◇. It is going to be an awkward hand, but I can wait for East's return at trick two before making my plans. The jack of hearts is won by the ace and East returns a heart.

It is possible already to reach a number of conclusions. East is likely to hold six hearts and, I imagine, five clubs, because West would probably have led a singleton club. I don't think East would have bid two notrumps, vulnerable, unless he held the ace of diamonds as well. In that case West's double must be based on the possession of five trumps.

Is there anything to be said for ruffing the heart return? No doubt I can restrict my trump losers to one by shortening my trumps, but if I ruff a good heart I shall almost certainly lose two diamond tricks.

It seems best to discard on the heart, enter hand by way of ace and another club, then lead a diamond, hoping that the jack will force the ace.

There's a snag about that, though. East will play a third club, and then it will be impossible to hold West to one trump trick.

But suppose I discard my singleton club now? Yes, that's better. Then I need play only one round of clubs before letting East in with the ace of diamonds.

I discard a club on the second heart, therefore, ruff a club, and finesse the jack of diamonds, losing to the ace. East returns a club, as good as anything for him. I discard one diamond on this trick and one on the king of hearts, arriving at this position:

♠ Q
♡ —
♢ K 6 2
♣ 8 5 4

♠ A K 9 8 5 4
♡ —
♢ 8
♣ —

Nothing can go wrong now. I cash the queen of spades, on which East, as expected, shows out. Then I play king of diamonds, ruff a diamond, and exit with the 8 of spades, end-playing West, who is down to ♠ J 10 x x. The full hand was:

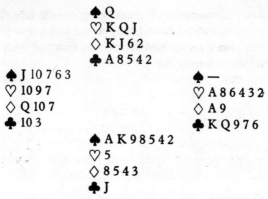

♠ Q
♡ K Q J
◇ K J 6 2
♣ A 8 5 4 2

♠ J 10 7 6 3
♡ 10 9 7
◇ Q 10 7
♣ 10 3

♠ —
♡ A 8 6 4 3 2
◇ A 9
♣ K Q 9 7 6

♠ A K 9 8 5 4 2
♡ 5
◇ 8 5 4 3
♣ J

Note that, although East was quite strong for his two notrump over-call, this bid had its usual effect of assisting the opposition.

Post-mortem

The critical play on this hand was the discard of the singleton club at trick two, averting the danger of a third round of clubs from East. This form of play, where declarer takes a discard in a suit of which dummy holds the master, occurs more often when a long suit is being established, as in this example:

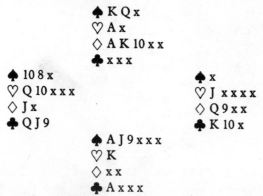

♠ K Q x
♡ A x
◇ A K 10 x x
♣ x x x

♠ 10 8 x
♡ Q 10 x x x
◇ J x
♣ Q J 9

♠ x
♡ J x x x x
◇ Q 9 x x
♣ K 10 x

♠ A J 9 x x x
♡ K
◇ x x
♣ A x x x

South is in six spades and West leads the queen of clubs. Declarer needs to establish a long diamond for his twelfth trick. After taking the club he must cash the king of hearts, cross to the ace of diamonds, and discard his second diamond on the ace of hearts. Then he can ruff a diamond low, play ace of spades and a spade to the king, and ruff the next diamond with the jack of spades, returning with a trump to make two more diamonds. If, instead, he begins with king of diamonds, ace of diamonds, and a diamond ruff, he will lose a trump trick either now or later. He cannot afford to ruff one diamond with the jack of spades and one with the ace.

13. Critical Stage

In an early round of the Gold Cup my team is in the familiar position of being a few points down to youthful opponents who have played an aggressive game. After some flat boards I pick up a hand that may decide the match:

♠ A 10 8 7 6 4 2   ♡ A K Q J 4   ◇ 5   ♣ —

We are vulnerable and I am fourth to speak. The opponent on my left opens **one spade** (!), my partner overcalls with **two clubs,** and the next player passes. I bid **two hearts** and partner responds with a cue-bid of the opponent's suit, **two spades.** I repeat my suit, **three hearts,** and he bids **four clubs.**

While my hand looked strong when I picked it up, there are two bad features. The spade opening on my left, probably a five-card suit, weakens my hand considerably, and it is also a disadvantage to be void of partner's suit. No doubt he has support for me, but I am not going to do anything rash at this critical stage. I bid simply **four hearts,** therefore, but he presses on with **five diamonds.** Having kept my head so far, I bid six hearts, which is passed out. It has been an improbable auction:

South	West	North	East
—	1♠	2♣	pass
2♡	pass	2♠	pass
3♡	pass	4♣	pass
4♡	pass	5◇	pass
6♡	pass	pass	pass

West leads the king of spades and the dummy is not what I was hoping to see:

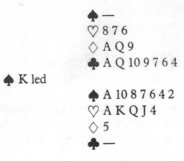

♠ —
♡ 8 7 6
◇ A Q 9
♣ A Q 10 9 7 6 4

♠ K led

♠ A 10 8 7 6 4 2
♡ A K Q J 4
◇ 5
♣ —

I certainly expected his hearts to be better than this; even the 10, as an entry card, would make a big difference.

The spades are probably 5 – 1, so I must get the clubs going somehow. Entries are the problem. Suppose I ruff the spade lead in dummy, play ace and another club, a diamond to the queen, and a third club. No good, because I can't get back to dummy.

Then suppose I can bring down the king of clubs in two rounds. Ace of clubs, club ruff, bringing down the king; draw trumps, diamond finesse, queen and another club, won by East, who will have to return a diamond to dummy's ace. That seems to work, and I don't see anything better.

I ruff the spade lead in dummy and play the ace of clubs, to which all follow. On the next club East plays the 8, and now I stop to consider, because I have another idea at the back of my mind. The position is:

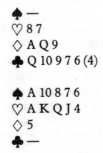

♠ —
♡ 8 7
◇ A Q 9
♣ Q 10 9 7 6 (4)

♠ A 10 8 7 6
♡ A K Q J 4
◇ 5
♣ —

If the clubs are 3 – 3, how am I going to make this contract? It would be all right if East held the king, but not if West holds it, because after club ruff, draw trumps, diamond to the queen, and a club losing to the king, West will exit with a spade and I shall be cut off from the table.

But I might ruff twice and contrive a throw-in against East by letting him win the third round of trumps. I am going to try that. I ruff with the jack of hearts and cash the ace and king, hoping that nobody will think of unblocking. Then I finesse the queen of diamonds and ruff a club with the queen, both opponents following suit. All depends now on East holding the third trump. I discard a diamond on the ace of spades and am happy to observe that East hesitates for a moment before discarding a diamond. When I exit with a low trump East wins and has to give dummy the lead in diamonds, the full hand being:

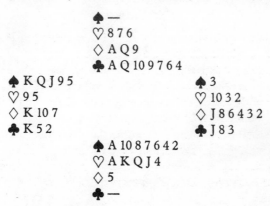

"I could have avoided that by unblocking the 10 of hearts," said East, much mortified.

Post-mortem

This was the situation after I had played off the top hearts, having previously ruffed with the jack:

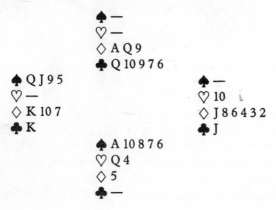

The continuation was: diamond finesse, club ruffed with the queen, ace of spades, low trump, forcing East to give dummy the lead.

As it turned out, it wasn't necessary to bid the slam to gain on the board. At the other table South took the view that the opening one spade was psychic and bid four spades on the first round. There was no way to avoid losing four trump tricks.

14. Long Distance

Elimination play in a suit contract generally leads to a situation where the declarer has trumps in both hands and the defenders are obliged either to lead into a tenace or to concede a ruff-and-discard. But it is not always like that; sometimes there are no trumps left in either hand after the elimination process.

In a qualifying round of Crockford's Cup, against opposition that does not appear to be especially formidable, I hold in second position:

♠ 3　♡ K 4　♢ Q 10 9 8 6 3　♣ J 8 7 2

We are vulnerable and East, on my right, opens **one spade.** They are playing the Precision system, so this should be a five-card suit in a limited hand. I pass and so does West. My partner reopens with **one notrump,** East passes, and I take out into **two diamonds.** West now enters with **two spades.** After two passes I compete with **three diamonds,** which becomes the final contract.

South	West	North	East
—	—	—	1♠
pass	pass	1NT	pass
2♢	2♠	pass	pass
3♢	pass	pass	pass

West leads the 9 of spades and partner puts down:

♠ K J 8 4
♡ J 5 3
♢ K J
♣ A K 10 5

♠ 9 led

♠ 3
♡ K 4
♢ Q 10 9 8 6 3
♣ J 8 7 2

North is somewhat above the normal range of 11 – 14 for one no-trump in the protective position. To double and follow with two

45

notrumps would be too much, so hands in the 15 – 17 range present a small problem. With some partners I play a convention whereby two clubs in the protective position may be either natural or 15 – 17 balanced. Responder may then bid the opponent's suit to discover the type. This method covers the awkward gap between a protective one notrump (11 – 14) and double, followed by two notrumps, (about 18 – 19).

Back to business. The 9 of spades is covered by the jack and queen. East lays down the ace of diamonds and follows with a second round, which I take in dummy.

This defence lights up the entire hand. East has played ace and another diamond because he did not like to lead a heart away from the queen. (It would have been better defence to put me to the heart guess before revealing the ace of diamonds.) No doubt, West's delayed raise was based on three trumps and the ace of hearts. Playing Precision, West might have passed the opening bid with an ace and a queen, but probably East has the queen of clubs. I am in danger of losing a spade, two hearts, a diamond and a club.

The general plan must be to force the opponents to open up the hearts. In dummy at trick four, I lead a spade and ruff, then draw the queen of diamonds. West follows suit, I throw a heart from dummy, and East discards a spade. We have arrived at this position:

♠ K 8
♡ J 5
♢ —
♣ A K 10 5

♠ —
♡ K 4
♢ 10 9
♣ J 8 7 2

As East has thrown a spade, I can eliminate this suit from both hands. I play a club to the ace, ruff a spade, cross to the king of clubs and ruff a fourth spade with my last trump. The queen of clubs is still out, but now I exit with a club, knowing that whoever wins the trick will be obliged to open up the hearts. As expected, East has the queen of clubs. He leads a heart, on which I play low. West wins with the ace and I make the rest of the tricks, the full hand being:

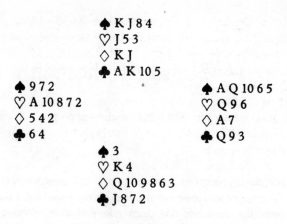

                ♠ K J 8 4
                ♡ J 5 3
                ♢ K J
                ♣ A K 10 5
    ♠ 9 7 2   ♠ A Q 10 6 5
    ♡ A 10 8 7 2   ♡ Q 9 6
    ♢ 5 4 2   ♢ A 7
    ♣ 6 4   ♣ Q 9 3
                ♠ 3
                ♡ K 4
                ♢ Q 10 9 8 6 3
                ♣ J 8 7 2

Post-mortem

The lead of a low spade from dummy at trick four was the first step in a long-distance elimination, designed to force the opponents to lead hearts. This was the position round the table after I had drawn trumps:

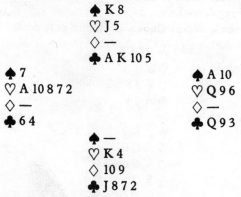

                ♠ K 8
                ♡ J 5
                ♢ —
                ♣ A K 10 5
    ♠ 7   ♠ A 10
    ♡ A 10 8 7 2   ♡ Q 9 6
    ♢ —   ♢ —
    ♣ 6 4   ♣ Q 9 3
                ♠ —
                ♡ K 4
                ♢ 10 9
                ♣ J 8 7 2

Once East had thrown a spade I could eliminate this suit from both hands and make the contract whether East or West held the guarded queen of clubs.

I thought at the time that East had made a tiny error in discarding a spade on the third trump, because if he keeps his spades, and I follow the same general line, he has a card of exit when in with the queen of clubs. However, there is another way to play the hand, which succeeds as the cards lie. Instead of ruffing out the spades, I exit with ace, king and jack of clubs, forcing East to lead away from the ace of spades or the queen of hearts.

47

15. Sinister Indication

Playing in a team event against first-class opposition, I pick up as dealer at game all:

♠ A K J 10 ♡ A Q 6 ◇ 10 7 6 4 3 ♣ 5

We are playing five-card majors in principle and my partner is a zealot on that point. However, the hand lacks reversing values and I don't fancy the sequence one diamond—two clubs—two diamonds. I am going to open **one spade**. He raises to **three spades** and I go to **four spades**.

South	West	North	East
1♠	pass	3♠	pass
4♠	pass	pass	pass

West leads the queen of clubs and partner puts down:

♠ 8 7 6 4
♡ 8
◇ K J 8 5 2
♣ A 6 4

♣ Q led

♠ A K J 10
♡ A Q 6
◇ 10 7 6 4 3
♣ 5

We are not indecently short of trumps, but it would be uncomfortable to take a losing finesse and be forced at once. After winning the first trick with the ace of clubs, therefore, I lead a spade to the ace, on which East plays the 5 and West the 2.

I can afford to lose two diamonds and a trump, so it must be right on general principles to establish the side suit early on. I lead a low diamond, on which the queen appears from West and the king is headed by the ace.

East considers the situation for some while, then plays a club, which I ruff. The position is now:

♠ 8 7 6
♡ 8
◇ J 8 5 2
♣ 6

♠ K J
♡ A Q 6
◇ 10 7 6 4
♣ —

If I lay down the king of spades and all follow, I shall make at least five without any difficulty. However, there are one or two sinister indications. West didn't lead his singleton diamond and East didn't give him a ruff. Also, on the first round of spades West played the 2, and both opponents normally play high-low when they hold three trumps. Adding one thing to another, I am inclined to place West with the three outstanding trumps. If that's right, and I play off the king of spades, West will ruff the next diamond, draw my last trump, and cash a club.

Despite the risk of ending up with only ten tricks instead of eleven, I play another diamond, on which West discards a heart.

Does that mean that West has no more trumps and began with two singletons? It's possible. But would it help me to finesse the jack of spades? Not really, because there is still a losing club in dummy. The safe play now is to ruff a club with the jack of spades and lay down the king. East shows out on the spade, so West makes two trump tricks, but that is all. This was the full hand:

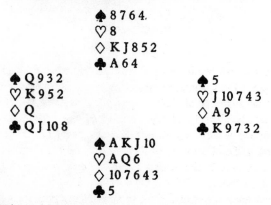

♠ 8 7 6 4
♡ 8
◇ K J 8 5 2
♣ A 6 4

♠ Q 9 3 2   ♠ 5
♡ K 9 5 2   ♡ J 10 7 4 3
◇ Q   ◇ A 9
♣ Q J 10 8   ♣ K 9 7 3 2

♠ A K J 10
♡ A Q 6
◇ 10 7 6 4 3
♣ 5

"You had only four spades," said my partner accusingly.

The defence put declarer under some pressure on this deal. After East had won with the ace of diamonds and returned the club, the position was:

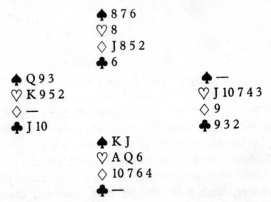

```
                    ♠ 8 7 6
                    ♡ 8
                    ◇ J 8 5 2
                    ♣ 6
    ♠ Q 9 3                        ♠ —
    ♡ K 9 5 2                      ♡ J 10 7 4 3
    ◇ —                            ◇ 9
    ♣ J 10                         ♣ 9 3 2
                    ♠ K J
                    ♡ A Q 6
                    ◇ 10 7 6 4
                    ♣ —
```

To play off the king of spades is fatal now. When instead I led a diamond, giving the defence a chance to ruff, West discarded a heart. To ruff the club now was fairly obvious, I suppose, and a diamond is also good enough; but it is slightly tempting to play a trump, and this loses the contract.

16. One Trump Is Enough

The final of Crockford's Cup is a multi-team event in which one plays short matches of ten boards, with a victory-point scale. In a match against one of the less fearsome teams I hold as dealer:

♠ K J 10 8 5　♡ A K 9 2　◇ 8 3　♣ K J

With both sides vulnerable, I open **one spade**. Partner responds **two diamonds**, I bid **two hearts**, and he puts me back to **two spades**.

I have a close decision now, as I see it. If you set the hand as a bidding problem, the answers would vary between three spades, three clubs, two notrumps, and pass.

At this form of scoring it is vital not to lose a game swing, especially against opponents one hopes to beat, so I am not going to pass. Two notrumps would be best if partner held something like Q x of spades and A x x of clubs, but bad if his clubs were x x x or any doubleton. Recalling a dictum of Adam Meredith that 5 – 4 – 2 – 2 is a suit and not a notrump distribution, I decide eventually in favour of **three spades**. Partner raises to **four spades**, seeming fairly happy.

South	West	North	East
1♠	pass	2◇	pass
2♡	pass	2♠	pass
3♠	pass	4♠	pass
pass	pass		

West leads the 4 of clubs and I see that at any rate we are in the best game contract.

```
              ♠ 7 6 4
              ♡ 6
              ◇ A K 7 5 4 2
              ♣ 10 5 2
  ♣ 4 led
              ♠ K J 10 8 5
              ♡ A K 9 2
              ◇ 8 3
              ♣ K J
```

East wins the first trick with the ace of clubs and promptly switches to ace and another spade.

He might have done this from A Q x, but to finesse the jack is unattractive for a number of reasons. If it loses, and a trump comes back, I shall have no play for the contract. It must be better to go up with the king, keeping a trump in dummy. West follows suit with the 9. The position is:

> ♠ 7
> ♡ 6
> ◇ A K 7 5 4 2
> ♣ 10 5

> ♠ J 10 8
> ♡ A K 9 2
> ◇ 8 3
> ♣ K

No problems now if the diamonds are 3 – 2; I can take three rounds of diamonds, play ace of hearts and ruff a heart, then discard my other heart loser on a winning diamond, losing only to the queen of trumps.

But of course, the diamonds may not be breaking. East's lead of ace and another trump at trick two rather suggests that he is not worried about my establishing the side suit. I don't need the three trumps in my hand; it might be a good idea to take a club ruff before testing the diamonds. With this in mind, I cash the king of clubs, cross to ace of diamonds, ruff a club, and only then play a diamond to the king. East shows out on this trick, discarding a club. We are down to:

> ♠ 7
> ♡ 6
> ◇ 7 5 4 2
> ♣ —

> ♠ J 10
> ♡ A K 9 2
> ◇ —
> ♣ —

I can't establish the diamonds, but I may get home on a crossruff. I ruff a diamond and follow with ace, king and another heart, ruffing on the table. Then I ruff another diamond with my last trump, and my losing heart and West's queen of spades fall together on the last trick. The full hand was:

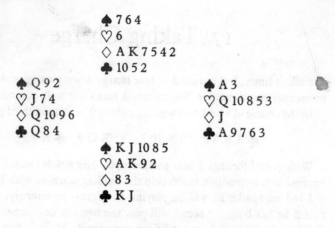

```
              ♠ 7 6 4
              ♡ 6
              ◇ A K 7 5 4 2
              ♣ 10 5 2
♠ Q 9 2                      ♠ A 3
♡ J 7 4                      ♡ Q 10 8 5 3
◇ Q 10 9 6                   ◇ J
♣ Q 8 4                      ♣ A 9 7 6 3
              ♠ K J 10 8 5
              ♡ A K 9 2
              ◇ 8 3
              ♣ K J
```

Post-mortem

East's defence of ace and another spade at trick two was not well conceived. If he simply returns a club, the hand will not develop at all well for the declarer.

The play of the king of clubs in the first diagram position, though simple in essence, was not at all obvious, I would say. This promotes two reflections, one of a general, one of a particular nature.

The general point is that, after he has seen that a 3 – 2 break in diamonds will give him the contract, declarer should not hastily pursue that line. On the contrary, he should assume that the diamonds are *not* breaking and should consider what he can do about that.

The particular, or technical, point concerns the management of the trumps. After two rounds the declarer had three trumps in his own hand, one in dummy. As he had no intention of drawing the master trump against him, it was sound tactics to reduce the trumps in his own hand; in the end, he was able to make all four separately.

17. Taking Charge

We all, at times, feel impelled to take charge when playing with a weak or inexperienced partner. Sometimes it turns out well, sometimes not.

In the course of a long and wearing rubber I pick up in third position:

♠ A K 8 2   ♡ K 10 7   ◇ K Q 9   ♣ A 4 2

With mixed feelings I hear partner open **one spade**; mixed feelings because it is impossible to develop the bidding sensibly with him, and if I bid six spades he will be playing it. Rightly or wrongly, I decide that if he has both red aces I will play the hand in notrumps. Bidding as he would himself, I respond **four notrumps**. He bids **five hearts**, two aces, and I press on with **five notrumps**. When he denies a king with **six clubs** I bid **six notrumps**, prepared to take the blame if seven is lay-down. The bidding is not recommended.

South	West	North	East
—	—	1♠	pass
4NT	pass	5♡	pass
5NT	pass	6♣	pass
6NT	pass	pass	pass

West leads the queen of clubs, and this is the dummy:

```
              ♠ Q 5 4 3
              ♡ A Q 8 5 2
              ◇ A 3
              ♣ 9 8

♣ Q led

              ♠ A K 8 2
              ♡ K 10 7
              ◇ K Q 9
              ♣ A 4 2
```

One spade he opens! Why is it that bad players so often choose the bid that increases the likelihood of their playing the hand?

Well, in case the suits don't break and I need a squeeze, I must duck the first trick. West continues with the jack of clubs, East completes an echo, and I win with the ace.

As five tricks in hearts will be enough in any event, I test the spades first. All follow to the ace and king; on the third round West discards a club, and on the fourth round West a club and East a diamond.

To complete the count, I play off three rounds of diamonds. On the third round West discards another club. There are only four cards left:

♠ —
♡ A Q 8 5
◇ —
♣ —

♠ —
♡ K 10 7
◇ —
♣ 4

Having gone through these motions, I may as well do some checking. West had two spades and two diamonds, and he has turned up with five clubs. There is only one club left, the king, and presumably East has that. So West has four hearts. If they are J 9 x x I can pick them up by leading the 10 first.

On the 10 of hearts West plays low without a flicker. But then, West is a good player, he knows the situation and wouldn't give me any indication. If the 10 loses to a singleton jack I can give up the game. It does lose. West almost falls off his chair with laughter; East, more polite, gathers in the jack of hearts and three diamonds with a puzzled air. This was the hand:

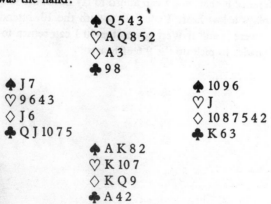

```
              ♠ Q 5 4 3
              ♡ A Q 8 5 2
              ◇ A 3
              ♣ 9 8
♠ J 7                         ♠ 10 9 6
♡ 9 6 4 3                     ♡ J
◇ J 6                         ◇ 10 8 7 5 4 2
♣ Q J 10 7 5                  ♣ K 6 3
              ♠ A K 8 2
              ♡ K 10 7
              ◇ K Q 9
              ♣ A 4 2
```

"Three down?" said my partner incredulously. "I think I could have made six spades."

"You would have made seven," I told him sadly. "Or seven hearts. Or seven notrumps, for that matter."

Post-mortem

At the time I thought I had played the hand like the original unlucky expert. It happens. Later came the horrible realisation that I could have avoided the trap I set for myself by following a slightly different sequence of play. Let's go back to the situation after the third round of spades:

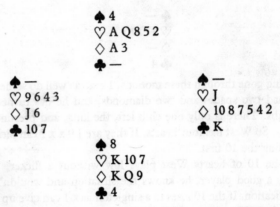

It costs nothing to play off three rounds of diamonds before the last spade. When West discards a club I can count him for 2 – 4 – 2 – 5. The difference is that now I can afford to lay down the king of hearts. If East plays a low heart I can follow with the 10, intending to run it if not covered; and if West covers the 10 I can return to hand with the 8 of spades to pick up the 9 6 of hearts.

18. Faintly Familiar

Most of the themes that one encounters in problems turn up at the table sooner or later. The difficulty is to recognise them in time.

Playing in a qualifying round of the Gold Cup, I am last to speak and hold:

♠ Q 5   ♡ 10 9 8 7 6 5 4   ◇ A   ♣ A Q 4

Both sides are vulnerable and West, on my left, opens **one spade.** My partner passes, East bids **one notrump,** and I enter with **two hearts.** West bids **two spades** and my partner raises to **three hearts.** My hand looks quite good after this trump support, so when East passes I go to **four hearts,** which is passed out.

South	West	North	East
—	1♠	pass	1NT
2♡	2♠	3♡	pass
4♡	pass	pass	pass

West leads the king of spades and I am glad to see that the first two cards partner lays down are the ace and king of trumps.

♠ 9 3
♡ A K 3
◇ Q J 10 6 4
♣ 9 7 6

♠ K led

♠ Q 5
♡ 10 9 8 7 6 5 4
◇ A
♣ A Q 4

West begins with king and ace of spades. East plays the 6 on the first round and on the second round the jack, after a slight shuffle. No doubt, his choice of the jack is meant to inform partner that he holds a high honour in diamonds, but not in clubs. So much the better. If the king of diamonds is on my right I can pick it up with a ruffing finesse and make five, unless the trumps are 3 – 0.

But West switches to the queen of hearts and suddenly I realise that everything in the garden is far from lovely. Whether he planned it or not, West has made a damaging assault on my entries to the table. Just look at the position after two tricks when West leads the queen of hearts:

♠ —
♡ A K 3
◇ Q J 10 6 4
♣ 9 7 6

♠ —
♡ 10 9 8 7 6 5 4
◇ A
♣ A Q 4

I can win with the king, cross to the ace of diamonds, return to dummy, and lead the queen of diamonds. But East will cover, and owing to the infuriating block in the trump suit I won't be able to get back to dummy and will be left with two losing clubs.

Some vague memory is stirring at the back of my mind, and just in time I refrain from calling for the ace of hearts. There was a hand once . . . Yes, I can let the queen of hearts hold. Then if West hasn't got another trump to lead I can play off the ace of diamonds before crossing to dummy.

West, looking a little puzzled, switches to a diamond, and the rest of the play is simple. I win with the ace, cross to the king of hearts, and take a ruffing finesse against the king of diamonds. This gives me the contract, the full hand being:

```
                    ♠ 9 3
                    ♡ A K 3
                    ◇ Q J 10 6 4
                    ♣ 9 7 6
♠ A K 10 7 4 2                        ♠ J 8 6
♡ Q                                   ♡ J 2
◇ 8 7 5                               ◇ K 9 3 2
♣ K 10 5                              ♣ J 8 3 2
                    ♠ Q 5
                    ♡ 10 9 8 7 6 5 4
                    ◇ A
                    ♣ A Q 4
```

"Well played," said my partner, gracious as always. "I don't know why it took you so long. There was a hand just like it in one of your own par contests."

Post-mortem

The deal to which my partner referred was part of a par contest for invited players, held at Selfridges in 1957. The hands were composed by Harold Franklin and myself, and this one was called "Curtsey to the Queen":

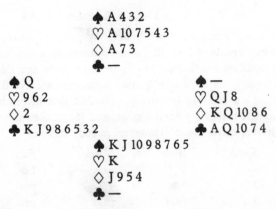

```
                  ♠ A 4 3 2
                  ♡ A 10 7 5 4 3
                  ◇ A 7 3
                  ♣ —
  ♠ Q                           ♠ —
  ♡ 9 6 2                       ♡ Q J 8
  ◇ 2                           ◇ K Q 10 8 6
  ♣ K J 9 8 6 5 3 2             ♣ A Q 10 7 4
                  ♠ K J 10 9 8 7 6 5
                  ♡ K
                  ◇ J 9 5 4
                  ♣ —
```

South plays in six spades after East has opened one diamond. West leads the 2 of diamonds. Declarer wins with the ace, crosses to the king of hearts and leads a low spade. West's queen is allowed to hold the trick, and whatever he plays next gives dummy the extra entry he needs to get the hearts going.

That hand, I remember, took ages to compose. It is interesting to see that the same basic theme—losing a trump trick unnecessarily to preserve an entry—can occur in a much more ordinary setting.

19. Remote Control

Sometimes one can finesse in trumps without leading them; or so it seems to the opposition.

At rubber bridge, with neither side vulnerable, I hold in fourth position:

♠ 10   ♡ A 9 6 3   ◇ A K J 9 7 2   ♣ Q 4

West, on my left, opens **one heart,** my partner passes, and East responds **one spade.** I overcall with **two diamonds** and West jumps to **three spades.** North raises to **four diamonds** and East passes. Before I have given the matter proper consideration, **five diamonds** slips out. It's a bad bid because (*a*) the fact that hearts have been bid on my left makes my hand weaker, and (*b*) partner may have had to stretch over three spades. However, nobody doubles.

South	West	North	East
—	1♡	pass	1♠
2◇	3♠	4◇	pass
5◇	pass	pass	pass

West leads the king of spades and dummy goes down with:

```
              ♠ J 7 4
              ♡ Q
              ◇ 10 6 5 3
              ♣ A 9 7 5 2
♠ K led
              ♠ 10
              ♡ A 9 6 3
              ◇ A K J 9 7 2
              ♣ Q 4
```

There is a spade and a club to lose on top, and as West opened one heart I cannot expect to ruff my losers with impunity. So, I shall have to develop the clubs. I have an idea that a switch to the king of hearts at trick two, preparing for an assault on dummy's entries, would be awkward for me, but fortunately West is no champion. He follows the king of spades with the ace, which I ruff.

On the ace of diamonds West shows out, discarding a heart. That's not surprising, because he raised to three spades without much in high cards. In any case, I must try to establish the clubs. I lead the queen and let it run. East wins with the king and leads a low heart. I take this with the ace, play a club to the ace, and ruff a club, to which all follow. Now dummy's clubs are good. After a heart ruff, on which East plays the jack, the position is:

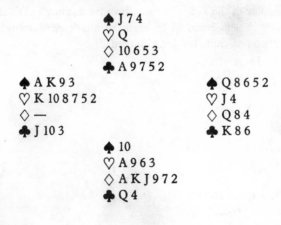

♠ J
♡ —
♢ 10 6
♣ 9 7

♠ —
♡ 9 6
♢ K J 9
♣ —

East still has Q 8 of diamonds, but the lead of a club from dummy is going to embarrass him. If he discards, so will I, and another club will follow. After a little thought he ruffs the club, I overruff and cash the king of diamonds. Now there is a trump and a club for my two heart losers. The full hand was:

        ♠ J 7 4
        ♡ Q
        ♢ 10 6 5 3
        ♣ A 9 7 5 2

♠ A K 9 3   ♠ Q 8 6 5 2
♡ K 10 8 7 5 2   ♡ J 4
♢ —   ♢ Q 8 4
♣ J 10 3   ♣ K 8 6

        ♠ 10
        ♡ A 9 6 3
        ♢ A K J 9 7 2
        ♣ Q 4

Post-mortem

This was not a complicated hand, but the situation at the finish was a little unusual:

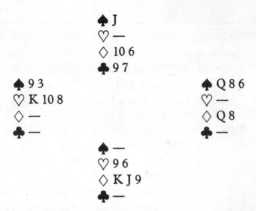

♠ J
♡ —
♢ 10 6
♣ 9 7

♠ 9 3　　　　　　　　　　　♠ Q 8 6
♡ K 10 8　　　　　　　　　♡ —
♢ —　　　　　　　　　　　　♢ Q 8
♣ —　　　　　　　　　　　　♣ —

♠ —
♡ 9 6
♢ K J 9
♣ —

East's trumps can be picked up by a straightforward finesse, but if declarer makes the mistake of leading a trump from dummy, East covers, and South is left in his own hand with two losing hearts. If he tries to ruff one of them he is overruffed and has to lose the last trick as well. Instead of finessing against East's queen of diamonds, South destroys it by remote control.

As I suspected at the time, a switch to the king of hearts at trick two would have been a killer. When East comes in with the king of clubs he leads the jack of hearts, forcing dummy to ruff. Declarer is then cut off from dummy's club winners. A first-class defender would have found this play of the king of hearts, because dummy's club suit looks dangerous and it is essential to begin an attack on dummy's entries before a round of clubs has been ducked.

20. Caution Justified

That engaging writer, S. J. Simon, who gave much thought to the psychological side of rubber bridge, used to say that bidding with bad partners was much easier than with good ones. If your man is going to play the hand you stay short of all close games or slams. If you are going to play the hand yourself you bid the borderline games but avoid doubtful slams, where failure would prolong the rubber.

My partner belongs to the category that Simon had in mind. After we have achieved vulnerability by a minor miracle, I pick up in third position:

♠ A Q 6 4 2   ♡ 10 8 4   ◇ A 6   ♣ 10 7 5

Partner opens **one diamond** and I respond **one spade**. There is a butt-in of **two clubs,** and after considering the matter from various angles my partner bids **three clubs,** a cue-bid of the enemy suit. For the moment I am not called upon to do more than repeat my fair suit, **three spades.** This is raised to **four spades.** Obviously I am worth a cue-bid of five diamonds now, but I reflect that (1) he won't co-operate intelligently in any slam try, (2) he has probably overbid already and doesn't realise it, and (3) I shall be happy to win the rubber. So, knowing that I shall have to take the blame if there are twelve or thirteen tricks on top, I pass, after this auction:

South	West	North	East
—	—	1 ◇	pass
1 ♠	2 ♣	3 ♣	pass
3 ♠	pass	4 ♠	pass
pass	pass		

West leads the king of clubs, and when the dummy goes down I see that my caution was justified.

$$\spadesuit K\,9\,5$$
$$\heartsuit A\,K\,6$$
$$\diamondsuit K\,10\,7\,4$$
$$\clubsuit A\,8\,3$$

♣ K led

$$\spadesuit A\,Q\,6\,4\,2$$
$$\heartsuit 10\,8\,4$$
$$\diamondsuit A\,6$$
$$\clubsuit 10\,7\,5$$

As I expected, his cue-bid of three clubs was quite unsound, though admittedly he had an awkward choice on the second round. Why he did not open one notrump is a mystery.

As West overcalled in clubs I put on the ace at once. East drops the 2, which suggests that the suit is breaking 6 – 1. If the trumps break I have ten tricks on top, and if East has four I can take two diamond ruffs in hand. But when I play off the ace and king of spades, East discards the 7 of hearts on the second round.

I am a trick short now, but it should be possible to develop a squeeze against East, who appears to have eleven cards in the red suits. Suppose I clear the spades and West cashes his club winners, then exits with a heart. I cash the other top heart, return to the ace of diamonds and play off the fifth trump. East will surely be squeezed at that point.

However, West is a first-class player and may not co-operate in this plan. For example, he may cash just one club, then switch to a diamond. That would threaten both the timing and entries for a squeeze.

I think a rare form of loser-on-loser may be more reliable. Suppose I let East win tricks in diamonds and meanwhile discard two clubs from my hand: then I can use the heart entries to ruff dummy's clubs, playing a sort of reverse dummy.

Pursuing this line, I play two top diamonds, West following suit, then a third diamond, on which I discard a club. In with the 9 of diamonds, East leads the jack, and I discard another club. The position is now:

♠ 9
♡ A K 6
◇ —
♣ 8 3

♠ Q 6 4
♡ 10 8 4
◇ —
♣ —

East exits with the queen of hearts, which runs to dummy's king. I ruff a club, cash the queen of spades, and lead another heart. It won't help West to ruff a loser, so he discards a club. I win with the ace of hearts and ruff the last club. Then my losing heart and West's jack of spades fall together on the last trick. The full hand was:

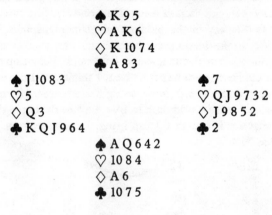

♠ K 9 5
♡ A K 6
◇ K 10 7 4
♣ A 8 3

♠ J 10 8 3
♡ 5
◇ Q 3
♣ K Q J 9 6 4

♠ 7
♡ Q J 9 7 3 2
◇ J 9 8 5 2
♣ 2

♠ A Q 6 4 2
♡ 10 8 4
◇ A 6
♣ 10 7 5

Post-mortem

It may seem that East would have done better to exit with the queen of hearts earlier, instead of playing the jack of diamonds, but then he is put in again with a diamond and must either give up a heart trick or concede a ruff-and-discard.

The declarer's stratagem of discarding two losers in preparation for an eventual trump coup was certainly unusual. The opportunity for such play occurs when the left-hand opponent has length in trumps as well as a long side suit. Looking at the North – South hands, it is odd to reflect that South made his contract by taking two *club* ruffs in hand!

21. A Wild Dash

My partner at rubber bridge is a newcomer to the club and his bidding is old-fashioned, not to say prehistoric. After some misadventures we stand at game all when I pick up as dealer:

♠ A K 8 3   ♡ 6   ◇ A J 8 6 2   ♣ A Q 5

I open **one diamond** and he responds **one notrump.** As in Auction bridge, this is a standard manœuvre on his part, covering a wide range of hands. I proceed with **two spades,** which appears to create a problem. I am expecting three hearts from him now, but after some reflection he puts me back to **three diamonds.**

What, as they say in the bidding competitions, should South call now? If you put the question to a panel the answers would include pass, three notrumps, four diamonds, and four clubs. Four clubs, giving a picture of the shortage in hearts, is best, I think, but I doubt whether my present partner would draw the right inferences. He might even pass. Finally, I make a wild dash to **five diamonds,** hoping there will be some play for it and that I can bring the rubber to an end. The bidding has been:

South	West	North	East
1◇	pass	1NT	pass
2♠	pass	3◇	pass
5◇	pass	pass	pass

West leads the 3 of hearts and the dummy earns a smile from the opposition:

♠ J
♡ A J 10 9 4
◇ 7 5 3
♣ 10 7 4 2

♡ 3 led

♠ A K 8 3
♡ 6
◇ A J 8 6 2
♣ A Q 5

Regretting my folly in not passing three diamonds, I win the first trick with the ace of hearts, play a spade to the ace and ruff a spade. About the only chance for the contract seems to be to find East with a doubleton K J of clubs, but when I lead a club from dummy he plays low.

Is there any hope now? I suppose West could have a singleton king of clubs. Then it might be possible to eliminate the spades and hearts and end-play East in the trump suit. (To finesse the queen of clubs and bring down the jack would produce the same effect, but this is less likely, as West might well have led a singleton jack.) It will probably lead to two down instead of one down, but I go up with the club ace and the king does fall.

Good so far, but to force East to lead away from the jack of clubs I have to eliminate the majors and find him with a doubleton honour in diamonds, K x or Q x or K Q. Well, he could be 4 – 2 – 2 – 5. I play off the ace of diamonds and all play low. After a spade ruff and a heart ruff, on which East drops the king, the remaining cards are:

♠ —
♡ J 10 4
♢ —
♣ 10 7 4

♠ K
♡ —
♢ J 8 6
♣ Q 5

When all follow to the king of spades, prospects are good. I exit with a low diamond; East wins and has to return a club, so I lose just two trump tricks. The full hand was:

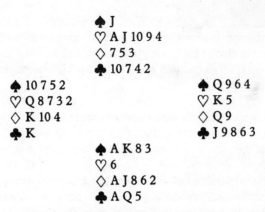

♠ J
♥ A J 10 9 4
♦ 7 5 3
♣ 10 7 4 2

♠ 10 7 5 2   ♠ Q 9 6 4
♥ Q 8 7 3 2   ♥ K 5
♦ K 10 4   ♦ Q 9
♣ K   ♣ J 9 8 6 3

♠ A K 8 3
♥ 6
♦ A J 8 6 2
♣ A Q 5

East reproaches himself for not unblocking with the queen of diamonds under the ace, and my partner tells me why over one diamond he responded one notrump in preference to one heart.

Post-mortem

This deal illustrates the familiar principle that when you are in a bad contract you must consider whether there is any lie of the cards that may enable you to make it. Here declarer must expect to lose two trump tricks (barring a possible K Q doubleton) and cannot afford to lose a club. When East follows with a low club on the first round the only chance is to drop a singleton honour that will leave East with a minor tenace.

It is possible to improve on declarer's play. Best is to lead a low diamond from dummy at trick two, before East can have any idea of the need to unblock a doubleton honour; and if it appears that either defender may have a doubleton K Q of diamonds there will be no need for any abnormal play in clubs.

22. Enter from the Wings

In a match against experienced opponents I am second to speak and hold:

♠ A 9 3   ♡ A K Q 8 6 4   ◇ A 6 5   ♣ Q

Our side is vulnerable and East, on my right, opens **one notrump,** described as 12 – 14. I **double** and West takes out into **two diamonds,** which is passed round to me. I have a close choice now, as I see it, between three hearts and three notrumps. Eventually I settle for **three hearts** and partner raises to **four hearts,** which is passed out. The bidding has been:

South	West	North	East
—	—	—	1NT
double	2◇	pass	pass
3♡	pass	4♡	pass
pass	pass		

West leads the 4 of diamonds and partner puts down:

♠ Q 7 2
♡ J 9 5
◇ 9 7 2
♣ K 8 5 2

◇ 4 led

♠ A 9 3
♡ A K Q 8 6 4
◇ A 6 5
♣ Q

Three notrumps would have been easier. I ought to have bid it instead of three hearts.

East plays the king of diamonds on the opening lead and returns the jack, which I take with the ace. All follow to the ace of hearts.

The king of clubs will take care of my losing diamond (assuming East has no more diamonds). The problem is to avoid losing two spades. There is not much prospect of end-playing East, because if I simply play out trumps he will keep K J of spades and a club. It would help if I could eliminate clubs, but I have only one sure entry to dummy.

As East opened one notrump and appears to have a doubleton diamond, there is not much chance of the hearts being 2 – 2. But perhaps East can be forced to provide me with an extra entry to the table? Yes, there may be something in that.

After one round of trumps I lead the queen of clubs. West plays the 7 and East, counting me for a singleton, puts on the ace.

At this point East has to give dummy an extra entry. He leads a heart, which runs to the 9. I play king of clubs and a ruff a club, return to the jack of hearts and lead the last club. East, who had unblocked the jack of clubs on the previous round, now plays a low one, so I ruff again, reaching this position:

♠ Q 7 2
♡ —
♢ 9
♣ —

♠ A 9 3
♡ K
♢ —
♣ —

I lead a low spade, intending if possible to duck into East's hand. West prevents this by going in with the 10. The queen loses to the king, but the 9 holds the next trick and I just make four hearts, the full hand being:

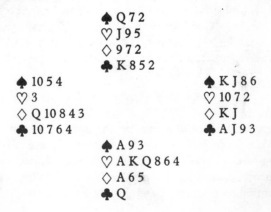

♠ Q 7 2
♡ J 9 5
♢ 9 7 2
♣ K 8 5 2

♠ 10 5 4
♡ 3
♢ Q 10 8 4 3
♣ 10 7 6 4

♠ K J 8 6
♡ 10 7 2
♢ K J
♣ A J 9 3

♠ A 9 3
♡ A K Q 8 6 4
♢ A 6 5
♣ Q

It would have been good play for East not to take the queen of clubs, but declarer can still succeed. He draws trumps and exits in spades, covering West's card. Now, if East lays down the ace of clubs, he is allowed to hold the trick, South discarding a diamond. East must then return a spade into the tenace or give dummy a trick with the king of clubs.

Problems in which declarer gives up a trump trick unnecessarily are common, but the manœuvre on this hand is seldom noticed. By giving East the lead after one round of trumps South created a situation in which East could not exit in trumps without giving the dummy an extra entry, needed here to eliminate the clubs. Here is a more striking example of the same form of play:

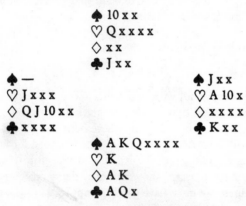

```
              ♠ 10 x x
              ♡ Q x x x x
              ♢ x x
              ♣ J x x
♠ —                          ♠ J x x
♡ J x x x                    ♡ A 10 x
♢ Q J 10 x x                 ♢ x x x x
♣ x x x x                    ♣ K x x
              ♠ A K Q x x x x
              ♡ K
              ♢ A K
              ♣ A Q x
```

Playing in six spades, South wins the diamond lead and plays a round of trumps, on which West shows out. Declarer cashes the second diamond, then exits with the king of hearts. East must win and is end-played, for whatever he plays, including a trump, gives an entry to the table, enabling South to discard one club on the queen of hearts and to take the club finesse.

71

23. For No Reward

Some important pairs events, especially international trials, are conducted on what is known as the Butler method. The scores returned at all tables on an individual board are added together, the mean is taken, called the "datum", and a pair obtains its own score by comparing with the average and translating into international match points. Thus, if the datum is plus 80 for North – South, and playing North – South you score 150, you are plus 70, which is 2 i.m.p. The idea is that the scoring should approximate more to team-of-four play, with game and slam swings having a proper reward.

Playing in an international trial scored on that basis, I hold as dealer, with neither side vulnerable:

♠ A K 6 3   ♡ A 9 7 6 4   ◇ 5   ♣ A 8 2

I open **one heart** and, with opponents silent, my partner responds **two diamonds.** Over **two spades** he gives me preference to **three hearts.** Any sequence of this kind, where both players have bid constructively, is forcing. As my club holding is not good for notrumps, I bid **four hearts.** Partner now advances to **five diamonds.** I take this to be a slam try in hearts, showing a good diamond suit but denying a control in clubs. He must have good trumps in that case, so I accept the invitation and bid **six hearts,** where we rest.

South	West	North	East
1♡	pass	2◇	pass
2♠	pass	3♡	pass
4♡	pass	5◇	pass
6♡	pass	pass	pass

West leads the jack of spades and partner goes down with:

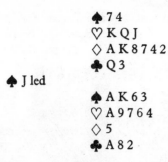

♠ 7 4
♡ K Q J
♢ A K 8 7 4 2
♣ Q 3

♠ J led

♠ A K 6 3
♡ A 9 7 6 4
♢ 5
♣ A 8 2

East plays the 5 of spades on his partner's jack and I win with the ace. To clarify the diamond position, I begin with ace, king, and a third diamond, on which East shows out. I ruff low and cross to the jack of hearts, the position at this stage being:

♠ 7
♡ K Q
♢ 8 7 4
♣ Q 3

♠ K 6 3
♡ A 9 7
♢ —
♣ A 8

On the fourth diamond East discards the 4 of clubs. Thinking that if the trumps are 4 – 1 it may be better to retain a low heart in hand, I ruff with the ace and lead the 7 to the queen. West drops the 10 of hearts and East follows suit. The situation deserves another look:

♠ 7
♡ K
♢ 8 7
♣ Q 3

♠ K 6 3
♡ 9
♢ —
♣ A 8

It is not necessary to draw the last trump, because if a diamond is ruffed I shall make my two trumps separately, regaining the trick at once. When I lead a diamond East ruffs and I overruff. After king and another spade the last diamond squeezes East, who began with four spades and the king of clubs. Thus I make an overtrick, the full hand being:

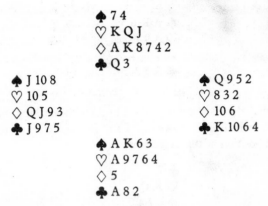

♠ 7 4
♡ K Q J
◇ A K 8 7 4 2
♣ Q 3

♠ J 10 8
♡ 10 5
◇ Q J 9 3
♣ J 9 7 5

♠ Q 9 5 2
♡ 8 3 2
◇ 10 6
♣ K 10 6 4

♠ A K 6 3
♡ A 9 7 6 4
◇ 5
♣ A 8 2

"The datum was 850 to North – South," my partner reported later. "We gain 160, 4 i.m.p. Nobody else made thirteen tricks, but the overtrick made no difference. Well done, though."

Post-mortem

This was the position at the finish:

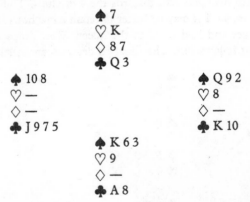

♠ 7
♡ K
◇ 8 7
♣ Q 3

♠ 10 8
♡ —
◇ —
♣ J 9 7 5

♠ Q 9 2
♡ 8
◇ —
♣ K 10

♠ K 6 3
♡ 9
◇ —
♣ A 8

Why did it help to lead the diamond instead of drawing the trump? The explanation is that after the diamond had been ruffed and over-ruffed, king of spades and a spade ruff left East in sole command of the spades. It was an unusual ending, but the deal does suggest that, more often than we realise, there can be an advantage in leaving a trump at large.

I didn't want to introduce a diversion in the middle of the narrative, but there was another very interesting feature in this hand. In the first diagram position it was a slight error to ruff with the ace. Best is to ruff with the 7, then play the 9 to the king, apparently blocking the trumps. But if they are 3 – 2, declarer continues with a diamond, as in the play described. If they are 4 – 1, East holding a heart more and a spade less, declarer can still make the contract: diamond ruffed and over-ruffed, king of spades and a spade ruff, good diamond; East ruffs and is left on play.

24. The Only Way

It has been a long and fiercely contested rubber, of not very high quality. We are game and 40, they game and 60, when in fourth position I pick up:

♠ Q 10 7 5 3   ♡ Q 10   ◇ A Q 5   ♣ K 10 6

After two passes East, on my right, opens **one club.** I overcall with **one spade,** which West **doubles** in a voice of thunder. My partner deliberates for a few moments before passing, and East passes. I was intending to remove myself into one notrump, but as partner hesitated over the double I had better pass and avoid any ethical query. So there we rest, after this bidding:

South	West	North	East
—	pass	pass	1♣
1♠	double	pass	pass
pass			

West leads the 4 of clubs and partner puts down:

```
              ♠ 6
              ♡ A 7 4 3
              ◇ J 9 4
              ♣ J 9 7 5 2
♣ 4 led
              ♠ Q 10 7 5 3
              ♡ Q 10
              ◇ A Q 5
              ♣ K 10 6
```

As I thought, we would have been better off in one notrump. He ought to have bid it—or at least passed at normal speed and left me free to do so.

The lead is surely a singleton and prospects are poor. To double at the one level when we have 40 below, West must have at least five spades, and it won't suit me at all if he is to make early trump tricks by ruffing clubs. One thought occurs to me. West has led the 4 of clubs, and if I drop the king under the ace East may conclude that his partner has led low from 10 6 4 and may not continue clubs.

That little scheme works. When the king of clubs falls under the ace, East switches to the 2 of hearts. I don't think he would lead from an unsupported king at this moment, having other alternatives, so I put in the 10 and am relieved to see West play the king. In dummy with the ace of hearts, I lead a low diamond to the queen. Once again, I am pleased to see West produce the king, as it leaves him on lead and also establishes an entry to dummy.

West exits with a heart, which runs to the queen. Now I want to make as many trumps as possible by ruffing. I play ace of diamonds, a diamond to the jack, and ruff a heart, to which all follow. We are down to six cards:

♠ 6
♡ 7
♢ —
♣ J 9 7 5

♠ Q 10 7 5
♡ —
♢ —
♣ 10 6

A club lead would allow West to shorten his trumps, relatively to mine, and I want to prevent this. East must hold the ace of spades, probably single, and if I play a spade now West will have to ruff the next trick and I will still have an exit card. A spade must be right, therefore. As expected, East wins with the ace and plays the jack of hearts. I discard a club and West is obliged to ruff and exit with the 9 of spades, which I win with the 10. Good heavens, I've got six tricks already and I'm going to make the contract! West, glaring at his partner, has to ruff the next club and concede the last trick to my queen of spades. This was the full hand:

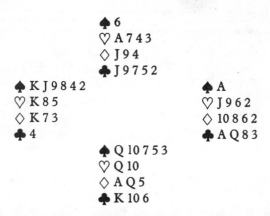

```
            ♠ 6
            ♡ A 7 4 3
            ◇ J 9 4
            ♣ J 9 7 5 2
♠ K J 9 8 4 2                    ♠ A
♡ K 8 5                         ♡ J 9 6 2
◇ K 7 3                         ◇ 10 8 6 2
♣ 4                             ♣ A Q 8 3
            ♠ Q 10 7 5 3
            ♡ Q 10
            ◇ A Q 5
            ♣ K 10 6
```

"That was the only way we could win the rubber on this deal," remarked my partner, before the defenders could get at each other's throats.

Post-mortem

The stratagem of dropping the king of clubs at trick one occurs more often when the distribution of the suit led is something like this:

```
            J 9 6 2
    5                   A Q 10 8 7 4
            K 3
```

East is marked with a long suit, so declarer can read the opening lead as a singleton. By dropping the king under the ace he may dissuade East from continuing the suit.

On the present hand the object was not just to prevent club ruffs, as such, but to prevent West from shortening his trumps. The importance of this can be seen if one looks again at the end position:

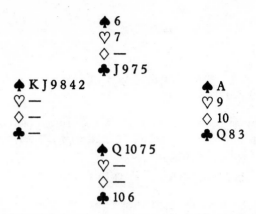

```
            ♠ 6
            ♡ 7
            ◇ —
            ♣ J 9 7 5
♠ K J 9 8 4 2              ♠ A
♡ —                       ♡ 9
◇ —                       ◇ 10
♣ —                       ♣ Q 8 3
            ♠ Q 10 7 5
            ♡ —
            ◇ —
            ♣ 10 6
```

Note that it would have been a mistake to lead a club at this point. West would ruff and lead a spade to the ace. After winning the next trick he exits with a low trump and has the tempo or, as chess players call it, the "opposition".

25. No Reaction

My opponents at rubber bridge are both experienced players, and my partner is at any rate not lacking in enterprise. With neither side vulnerable, I hold in second position:

♠ 6 3   ♡ Q 5 4 2   ◇ Q 10 3   ♣ Q 10 5 2

East, on my right, opens **three spades,** I pass, and West appears to give his hand a moment's thought before he, too, passes. If my partner has noticed this hesitation it has not deterred him, for he is evidently contemplating some action. Eventually he **doubles** and the opener passes.

A little nervous about the way things are going, I bid **four clubs** in preference to four hearts. It is less likely to be doubled and gives us more space to find the best spot. I am relieved to hear West bid **four spades,** which I dare say we can beat, but partner is not finished. On the contrary, he bids **six clubs,** which is passed out. It has been a surprising auction:

South	West	North	East
—	—	—	3♠
pass	pass	double	pass
4♣	4♠	6♣	pass
pass	pass		

West leads the 4 of spades and partner begins by displaying J 6 4 3 of clubs and passing on to the next suit. When this hoary jest obtains no reaction, he lets us see the remainder:

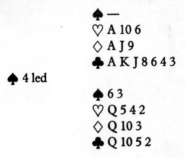

```
              ♠ —
              ♡ A 10 6
              ◇ A J 9
              ♣ A K J 8 6 4 3

♠ 4 led

              ♠ 6 3
              ♡ Q 5 4 2
              ◇ Q 10 3
              ♣ Q 10 5 2
```

Well, there are chances. I need to find the diamond finesse and lose only one heart. The first step, obviously, is to draw trumps and eliminate the spades. I ruff the opening lead with the 6 of clubs and play a trump to the 10, on which East discards a spade. The second spade is ruffed high and the last trump is drawn.

As I am short of entries to my own hand and want to tempt a cover, I lead the queen of diamonds. West covers without much thought and all follow to two more rounds of diamonds, West playing the 6 and 8. That leaves:

<pre>
          ♠ —
          ♡ A 10 6
          ◇ —
          ♣ A J 4

          ♠ —
          ♡ Q 5 4 2
          ◇ —
          ♣ 5 2
</pre>

Now, what's the best way to manage the hearts? First, can I tell how they are divided? Trumps are known to be 2 – 0; spades probably 7 – 4; diamonds 4 – 3, but who has the missing diamond?

There's a fair clue to this. When I led the queen, West, though he could see A J 9 on the table, seemed quite happy about covering with the king. If he had held K x x x he would have given the matter some consideration, because if declarer held Q 10 x x the cover would be a mistake. If I am right in thinking that West had only three diamonds, his distribution is 4 – 4 – 3 – 2.

West probably has the king of hearts, but the jack could be on either side. I could cross to dummy and try a low heart, intending to duck the trick to West, but that would depend on East failing to cover the 6.

There must be some answer to this. Yes, what about running the queen? If East has the king he will be on play. If West covers the queen with the king? Still all right.

I lead the queen, which is covered by the king and ace. Back to the 5 of clubs for another heart lead. West plays the 9 and I put on the 10. East wins and gives in, as he has to concede a ruff-and-discard. The full hand was:

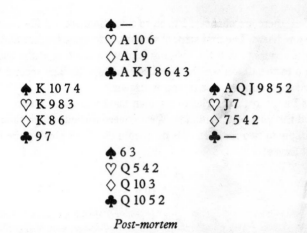

```
                    ♠ —
                    ♡ A 10 6
                    ◇ A J 9
                    ♣ A K J 8 6 4 3
  ♠ K 10 7 4                        ♠ A Q J 9 8 5 2
  ♡ K 9 8 3                         ♡ J 7
  ◇ K 8 6                           ◇ 7 5 4 2
  ♣ 9 7                             ♣ —
                    ♠ 6 3
                    ♡ Q 5 4 2
                    ◇ Q 10 3
                    ♣ Q 10 5 2
```

Post-mortem

As the cards lie, ace of hearts followed by a low one would have been good enough, but this would fail, obviously, against K J x x in the West hand.

It had not struck me before that with A 10 x opposite Q x x x there was a perfect elimination whenever the suit was divided 4 – 2. If the player on declarer's left has the doubleton, the play is ace, then low to the queen; if West holds K x he is endplayed.

The same sort of manœuvre is available when declarer holds any variation of this common holding:

A J x
10 x x x

When the conditions for an elimination ending are present, declarers usually play ace and another, which wins when either defender has a doubleton honour. But if East is unlikely to hold more than three cards, there is a stronger line. Begin by leading the 10; if this is covered, win with the ace, return to hand, and lead up to the J x. This wins not only when East has K x or Q x, but also when he has x x, x x x, or K Q x.

26. Narrow Escape

Sometimes one misses a play that is not at all complicated, and afterwards one wonders, was it just a blind spot or might other players have missed it as well?

In the course of a long rubber I pick up in second position:

♠ J 8 6 3 2   ♡ Q 9 7 6   ◇ 7 3   ♣ 6 2

It is game all and after two passes West, on my left, opens **one spade,** my partner **doubles,** and East bids **one notrump.** West bids **two spades,** my partner **doubles** again, and East passes. I have to bid **three hearts,** and all pass. The bidding has been:

South	West	North	East
—	—	—	pass
pass	1♠	double	1NT
pass	2♠	double	pass
3♡	pass	pass	pass

West leads the king of spades and this dummy goes down:

```
            ♠ 7 4
            ♡ A J 8 5 3
            ◇ A 10 8 5
            ♣ A Q
♠ K led
            ♠ J 8 6 3 2
            ♡ Q 9 7 6
            ◇ 7 3
            ♣ 6 2
```

"At least you have chosen a good suit," my partner remarks. Yes, indeed! I wonder what he would have done if I had been obliged to respond three clubs, perhaps on four small.

West follows the king of spades with the queen, East discarding the 4 of clubs. After some thought West switches to the king of hearts.

That's good in a way—no trump loser—but I can't be sure about the club finesse and I must organise diamond ruffs. After winning with

83

the ace of hearts I play a low diamond from the table. East goes in with the queen and plays a second heart, on which West discards a club. The position is:

$$\spadesuit\ -$$
$$\heartsuit\ J\,8\,5$$
$$\diamondsuit\ A\,10\,8$$
$$\clubsuit\ A\,Q$$

$$\spadesuit\ J\,8\,6$$
$$\heartsuit\ Q\,7$$
$$\diamondsuit\ 7$$
$$\clubsuit\ 6\,2$$

I have lost three tricks and there is one trump out, the 10. Suppose I play to ruff two diamonds. I can play a diamond to the ace and ruff a diamond, then a club to the ace and ruff the last diamond. At that point a club to the queen will be safe if East has the king, but if West takes this trick he will play another spade, promoting his partner's trump, and I shall look exceedingly foolish. On the other hand, if I finesse the queen of clubs, and it loses, East will return his third heart and I shall be a trick short.

Who *has* got the king of clubs? Having a singleton spade, East might have bid one notrump on the K Q J of diamonds and the J 10 of clubs. But equally, there is room for him to hold the king of clubs.

I don't have to decide at once. I play a diamond to the ace and ruff a diamond, East producing the king on the third round and West the 9. The jack is still out. I think East must have it, for with 1 – 3 – 3 – 6 distribution he would have bid two clubs over the double rather than one notrump.

If East has K Q J x of diamonds, the king of clubs could be with West. I take out a club—and put it back.

I had been looking at the jack of hearts, and of course there's a better solution. I can make a certainty of the contract by ruffing a spade with the jack of hearts, the last diamond with the queen of hearts, then a spade with the 8. East may overruff but will have to return a club; away from the king, as it turns out, the full hand being:

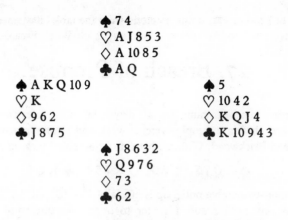

♠ 7 4
♡ A J 8 5 3
◇ A 10 8 5
♣ A Q

♠ A K Q 10 9   ♠ 5
♡ K   ♡ 10 4 2
◇ 9 6 2   ◇ K Q J 4
♣ J 8 7 5   ♣ K 10 9 4 3

♠ J 8 6 3 2
♡ Q 9 7 6
◇ 7 3
♣ 6 2

Post-mortem

That was a narrow escape. For some reason, the trump throw-in was elusive; at least, I found it so. This was the position after I had ruffed the third diamond:

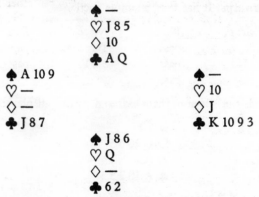

♠ —
♡ J 8 5
◇ 10
♣ A Q

♠ A 10 9   ♠ —
♡ —   ♡ 10
◇ —   ◇ J
♣ J 8 7   ♣ K 10 9 3

♠ J 8 6
♡ Q
◇ —
♣ 6 2

To lead a club to the ace, ruff a diamond, and exit with a club, would win as the cards lie, but would lose if West held the king of clubs. The sure play was to ruff a spade with the jack of hearts, a diamond with the queen, then lead another spade and ruff with the 8. If East does not overruff he can be thrown in with the last trump.

West's object in leading the king of hearts at trick three was to make it more difficult for the declarer to take diamond ruffs in his own hand. The more natural defence of a club would have worked better.

27. Breach of Promise

My partner in a pairs game is a fair player, but not a tournament 'pro', so we are playing a simple system: weak and strong notrump, two clubs, and Blackwood. With neither side vulnerable I pick up as dealer:

♠ A Q J 5   ♡ 8 3   ◇ K 7 5 4   ♣ K Q 8

Our non-vulnerable notrump is officially 13 – 15, but the doubleton heart is unattractive and I prefer to open **one diamond**. Partner responds **one heart**. Some players consider it a breach of promise to by-pass the spade suit in this sort of sequence, but the hand fits well into the range of a one notrump rebid (he will expect 15 – 16), and there is often advantage in suppressing the strong tenace holding in a major suit. At any rate, I rebid **one notrump** and this is raised to **three notrumps.** It has been a simple auction:

South	West	North	East
1◇	pass	1♡	pass
1NT	pass	3NT	pass
pass	pass		

West leads the queen of diamonds and partner displays:

♠ 7 4
♡ Q 10 6 5
◇ A 2
♣ A 10 7 5 3

◇ Q led

♠ A Q J 5
♡ 8 3
◇ K 7 5 4
♣ K Q 8

As West has led my suit, no doubt his diamonds are long and strong. I have to consider whether or not to hold off the first trick.

By holding off I would make it more difficult for the opposition to establish their diamonds, but there are two reasons against it. One is that if the spade finesse is right and the clubs break, the contract will be unbeatable; in that case it might be a mistake to give West a chance to switch to a low heart from A x x or K x x, or to a perspicacious 9 from A 9 x. Secondly, if the clubs are not solid I may need the ace of diamonds later as an entry to the table.

I decide to win the first diamond, therefore, and lead the king of clubs. West drops the 9, which is slightly sinister; and when I follow the queen of clubs he discards a low spade. That's not so good. The position at the moment is:

♠ 7 4
♡ Q 10 6 5
◇ A
♣ A 10 7 5

♠ A Q J 5
♡ 8 3
◇ 7 5 4
♣ (Q) 8

I can clear the clubs, but when East comes in with the jack he will knock out the ace of diamonds and I will be short of entries to take two finesses in spades.

But wait a moment! As the 10, 8 and 7 of clubs are equals, I can afford to overtake the queen of clubs. Noting with relief that I have not called for a card from dummy, I overtake with the ace and finesse the queen of spades successfully. Then the 8 of clubs is headed by the 10, forcing the jack from East, who returns a diamond to dummy's ace. After cashing the two clubs I finesse the jack of spades with fair confidence, and the ace of spades is my ninth trick. The full hand was:

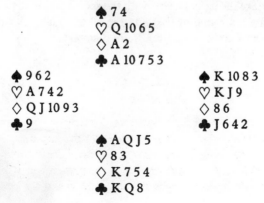

♠ 7 4
♡ Q 10 6 5
◇ A 2
♣ A 10 7 5 3

♠ 9 6 2   ♠ K 10 8 3
♡ A 7 4 2   ♡ K J 9
◇ Q J 10 9 3   ◇ 8 6
♣ 9   ♣ J 6 4 2

♠ A Q J 5
♡ 8 3
◇ K 7 5 4
♣ K Q 8

There was nothing very profound in the play of this hand but the overtaking play in clubs might have been overlooked. I derived inspiration from a deal in the European Championship some years ago, which was something like this:

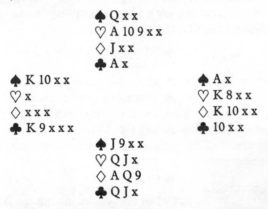

♠ Q x x
♡ A 10 9 x x
♢ J x x
♣ A x

♠ K 10 x x
♡ x
♢ x x x
♣ K 9 x x x

♠ A x
♡ K 8 x x
♢ K 10 x x
♣ 10 x x

♠ J 9 x x
♡ Q J x
♢ A Q 9
♣ Q J x

Playing in three notrumps, South won the club lead with the queen and led the queen of hearts, which was allowed to hold. He followed with the jack of hearts, playing low from dummy when West discarded a diamond. East took the heart and forced out the ace of clubs. Declarer used this entry to lead the jack of diamonds, and with the aid of the double finesse in this suit he made game with four hearts, three diamonds and two clubs.

If East had allowed the jack of hearts to hold, South would have been an entry short for the two diamond finesses. His correct play was to overtake the jack of hearts with the ace, finesse in diamonds, and then play a third round of hearts to the 10 and king, with the ace of clubs as entry for the second finesse in diamonds.

28. Telescoping the Trumps

Playing rubber bridge at a table where all the players know their way around, I hold in fourth position:

♠ J 9 8 7 6 4   ♡ A 10 5   ◇ A 6   ♣ J 8

Neither side has scored a game, but we have a part score of 40. West, on my left, opens **one notrump,** presumptively 12 – 14, and when this comes round to me I venture **two spades.** After two passes East competes with **three diamonds.** My partner, in turn, raises me to **three spades,** and when this reaches West, he **doubles.** There we rest, after this auction:

South	West	North	East
	1NT	pass	pass
2♠	pass	pass	3◇
pass	pass	3♣	pass
pass	double	pass	pass
pass			

West leads the king of clubs and dummy goes down with:

> ♠ A 5
> ♡ K J 6 2
> ◇ 8 4 3
> ♣ Q 7 6 2

♣ K led

> ♠ J 9 8 7 6 4
> ♡ A 10 5
> ◇ A 6
> ♣ J 8

East plays the 3 of clubs on his partner's king and West switches to the 5 of diamonds. East puts on the king and I win with the ace.

There seem to be five more or less certain losers—two trumps, two clubs and a diamond. I can play for one down by leading trumps and discarding a heart eventually on the queen of clubs.

89

But before I surrender, are there any reasonable chances of making the contract? West's spades need not be better than K Q x; with the A K of clubs, that would be enough for his double of three spades (we are 40 up, remember). If the trumps are like that—K Q x opposite 10 x—I may be able to set up one of those positions where a loser is discarded and neither opponent can ruff without sacrificing a trump trick. It risks going two down, but it's worth trying.

What about the queen of hearts? As West is marked with A K of clubs and, to judge from the play, the queen of diamonds, and I hope to find him with K Q x of spades, I must place East with the queen of hearts.

The first step is to lead the jack of spades. West covers with the queen, the ace wins, and East drops the 3. I finesse the 10 of hearts successfully, and all follow to the ace and king. All well so far; the remaining cards are:

♠ 5
♡ J
♢ 8 4
♣ Q 7 6

♠ 9 8 7 6 4
♡ —
♢ 6
♣ J

When I lead the thirteenth heart from dummy, East gives the matter some thought. That's encouraging, because it suggests that his remaining trump is the 10. Eventually he discards a club. I was intending to discard my second diamond, but that could be a mistake now: West might ruff low, cash the ace of clubs, and give East a ruff with the 10 of spades. So I throw my second club and West, as expected, ruffs with the 2. The defenders take their diamond trick, but the remaining trumps fall together and I make the contract for the loss of two trumps, one diamond, and one club. The full hand was:

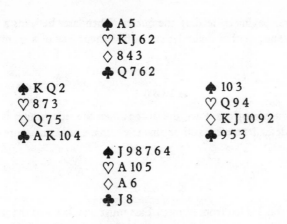

                    ♠ A 5
                    ♡ K J 6 2
                    ◇ 8 4 3
                    ♣ Q 7 6 2
    ♠ K Q 2   ♠ 10 3
    ♡ 8 7 3   ♡ Q 9 4
    ◇ Q 7 5   ◇ K J 10 9 2
    ♣ A K 10 4   ♣ 9 5 3
                    ♠ J 9 8 7 6 4
                    ♡ A 10 5
                    ◇ A 6
                    ♣ J 8

Post-mortem

The defenders were in a well known dilemma when the last heart was led:

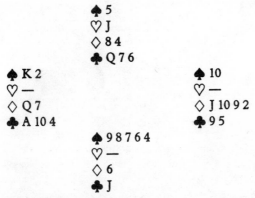

                    ♠ 5
                    ♡ J
                    ◇ 8 4
                    ♣ Q 7 6
    ♠ K 2   ♠ 10
    ♡ —   ♡ —
    ◇ Q 7   ◇ J 10 9 2
    ♣ A 10 4   ♣ 9 5
                    ♠ 9 8 7 6 4
                    ♡ —
                    ◇ 6
                    ♣ J

Whether East ruffs with the 10 or West with the 2, the defence can make only one trump trick thereafter.

The simplest situation of this kind occurs when one defender has K x of the trump suit and the other the singleton ace. There are some other combinations for which it is well to be prepared:

                    A 4
    K 10 3   J 6
                    Q 9 8 7 5 2

Declarer begins by leading the queen. When later he leads a winner in a side suit, neither defender can ruff without loss of a trump trick.

753

KQ   J94

A 10 8 6 2

Here the ace brings down the queen; then the side winner is played and the defenders, after ruffing this trick, make only one more trump.

642

QJ   A93

K 10 8 5 4

When the 2 is led from dummy East must play low and the jack falls under the king. Once again, neither defender can ruff a side winner without loss of a trump trick.

29. In Passing

The Waddington Cup for Life Masters Pairs does not carry quite the same prestige as when entry was by invitation, but it remains one of the best events in the calendar. Playing one year against one of those pairs from the Midlands who seem to amass a large number of master points, I hold in fourth position:

♠ A ♡ 7542 ◇ A K J 9 ♣ J 9 8 3

Our side is vulnerable and after two passes East, on my right, opens **one club.** In a pairs one has to take part in the auction if possible, so I overcall with **one diamond.** West bids **one spade** and my partner enters with **two clubs,** the enemy suit. This is what we call an "unassuming cue-bid". Initially, it shows the values for a raise in diamonds, based on high cards as well as some trump support. After a pass by the opener I bid **two diamonds,** indicating no wish to advance. When this comes round to him, East contests with **two spades.** North in turn goes to **three diamonds,** which buys the contract. It has been a typical pairs auction:

South	West	North	East
—	pass	pass	1♣
1◇	1♠	2♣	pass
2◇	pass	pass	2♠
pass	pass	3◇	pass
pass	pass		

West leads the king of spades and partner puts down a fair hand:

```
                    ♠ J 8 6 2
                    ♡ A Q 6
                    ◇ 7 6 4 2
                    ♣ A 5

        ♠ K led
                    ♠ A
                    ♡ 7 5 4 2
                    ◇ A K J 9
                    ♣ J 9 8 3
```

We have the balance of the cards, but they have pushed us. It will be a horrible result if I don't make the contract.

East plays a low spade on the first trick and I win with the ace. Drawing trumps won't give me enough tricks, so I begin by running the 8 of clubs. West plays the 7 and East wins with the 10. Divining my general intention, East switches to the queen of diamonds, which I take with the ace. He would have led low from Q x, so the queen is probably a singleton.

Pursuing the idea of making the trumps separately, I play a club to the ace, ruff a spade with the 9 of diamonds, and lead a third club. West, after some consideration, ruffs with the 8 and I discard the 6 of hearts from dummy. West exits with a trump and East, as expected, discards a club. The position is:

```
                    ♠ J 8
                    ♡ A Q
                    ◇ 7 6
                    ♣ —

                    ♠ —
                    ♡ 7 5 4 2
                    ◇ K
                    ♣ J
```

I have lost two tricks, West still has the 10 of diamonds, and East must have the king of hearts for his opening bid. If I draw the trump I shall make only the ace of hearts and the last trump, so far as I can see. It must be better to lead the jack of clubs, because if West goes in with the 10 of diamonds I can throw a heart from dummy and make my three trumps separately.

West studies the jack of clubs for a while but finally makes the good play of discarding a spade. I ruff on the table and now we are down to:

♠ J 8
♡ A Q
◇ 7
♣ —

♠ —
♡ 7 5 4 2
◇ K
♣ —

Only one trick since the last diagram, but a new situation. I am still going to make both remaining trumps. I ruff a spade with the king of diamonds, lead a heart to the ace, and exit with the queen. This leaves East on lead at trick 12, and whatever he plays I am going to make dummy's last trump *en passant*. The full hand was:

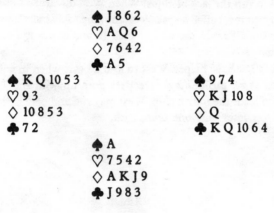

♠ J 8 6 2
♡ A Q 6
◇ 7 6 4 2
♣ A 5

♠ K Q 10 5 3   ♠ 9 7 4
♡ 9 3   ♡ K J 10 8
◇ 10 8 5 3   ◇ Q
♣ 7 2   ♣ K Q 10 6 4

♠ A
♡ 7 5 4 2
◇ A K J 9
♣ J 9 8 3

Post-mortem

It was a pretty and unusual ending:

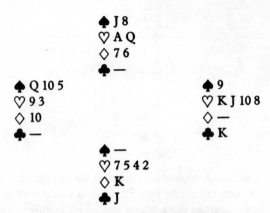

Note, first, that it would not be good play to draw the outstanding trump while there was still some ruffing to be done. Also, West was right not to ruff the jack of clubs. When West discarded a spade, South ruffed in dummy, ruffed a spade with the king of diamonds and exited in hearts, leaving East in the lead at trick 12 and ensuring a trick for the 7 of diamonds.

It would not have helped West to lead a heart when in with the 8 of diamonds at an earlier stage. Declarer goes up with the ace, ruffs a spade, and leads the fourth club. West may ruff and play his last trump, but declarer loses only one more trick.

30. Blind Alley

In a pairs event at a London Congress I am playing with a partner who is known to indulge in flights of fancy. As dealer, with both sides vulnerable, I hold:

♠ K Q 6 3   ♡ K Q J 6 2   ◇ K 6 4   ♣ 5

I open **one heart** and the partner responds **one spade**. My playing values justify a raise to **three spades**. Partner now bids **three no-trumps**. That makes me doubtful about his spade suit. Fortunately, I don't have to guess between four spades and a pass, I can test him out with **four hearts**. This he passes hurriedly. It has been an unusual sequence:

South	West	North	East
1♡	pass	1♠	pass
3♠	pass	3NT	pass
4♡	pass	pass	pass

West leads the jack of diamonds and partner goes down with:

♠ A 8 4
♡ 10 7 3
◇ Q 8 3
♣ A 8 6 2

◇ J led

♠ K Q 6 3
♡ K Q J 6 2
◇ K 6 4
♣ 5

Digressing for a moment, I don't mind a semi-psychic response on A x x provided that it solves a temporary problem and will be manageable thereafter. It is true that North has an awkward response over one heart, being midway between one notrump and a natural two notrumps. However, one spade will do nothing to close the gap. Suppose my next bid is two of any suit: in each case North will have a borderline decision. His best bid over one heart is two clubs; then, having responded at the two level, he can afford to make a minimum call on the next round, passing two hearts or giving simple preference over two diamonds.

Still, we seem to have landed on our feet, as the hands fit well and four hearts is a reasonable contract. On the first trick East goes up with the ace of diamonds and returns the 2, which I take with the king. Clearly East has a doubleton A x and a ruff is threatened. I try a low heart, but West goes in with the ace and gives his partner the expected ruff in diamonds. East exits with the 10 of spades. I win with the king and lead a high heart, on which East discards a club. The position is now:

♠ A 8
♡ 10
♢ —
♣ A 8 6 2

♠ Q 6 3
♡ Q J 6
♢ —
♣ 5

There is still one trump out and I have to take care of the fourth spade. The usual safety play (extra chance play, really) in this sort of situation is to tackle the side suit before drawing the last trump, playing for the same opponent to hold the long trumps and the long spades. But that can hardly gain here. West has turned up with five diamonds and three hearts, he can hardly hold four spades as well.

If anyone has four spades, it is surely East. In that case he will be 4 – 2 – 2 – 5. Perhaps I can put him under some pressure in the black suits. I play a club to the ace and ruff a club high, then lead a low heart to the 10. This seems to embarrass East. Yes, it would; he is down to three spades and two clubs and is caught in a trump squeeze. Eventually he throws a spade and I make the rest of the tricks, the full hand being:

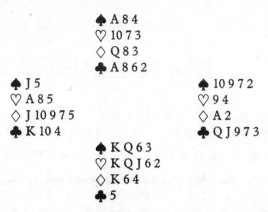

"You see," my partner pointed out, "my one spade bid helped us to get to game."

Post-mortem

This was the situation round the table after the second round of trumps:

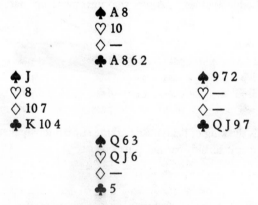

At this point declarer had to realise (1) that to try for a spade ruff, placing West with four spades, was a blind alley, and (2) that to squeeze East in the black suits would be possible only if West could be deprived of club control. The continuation was: club to the ace and club ruff, followed by a heart to the 10, squeezing East.

Whether the ending should properly be called a ruffing squeeze is open to argument (for those who like to argue about such things). At any rate, one of the threats against East was that a club trick would be established by ruffing.

31. Trap for the Unwary

My partner at rubber bridge is a trier but not very quick-witted at the game. With both sides vulnerable, I pick up as dealer:

♠ —   ♡ Q 10 8 3   ◇ A K 8 5 3   ♣ A Q 10 7

I open **one diamond** and partner responds **one spade**. Resisting a temptation to be the first to declare notrumps, I rebid **two clubs**. This simple sequence appears to create a problem. After a while partner raises to **three clubs**. It may be unwise, but I am going to try **three notrumps**.

Once again, partner seems to be puzzled. He frowns, strokes his chin, consults the ceiling, and finally transfers to **four spades**. I expect he is 6 – 1 – 2 – 4 and doesn't trust me to hold the hearts. Well, I can't bear to watch him go 300 down in four spades, so I go to **five clubs**. Nobody doubles, despite the unconvincing nature of the auction:

South	West	North	East
1◇	pass	1♠	pass
2♣	pass	3♣	pass
3NT	pass	4♠	pass
5♣	pass	pass	pass

West leads the king of hearts. Remarking superfluously that he found his hand difficult to bid, partner puts down:

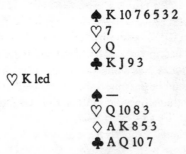

```
                    ♠ K 10 7 6 5 3 2
                    ♡ 7
                    ◇ Q
                    ♣ K J 9 3
      ♡ K led
                    ♠ —
                    ♡ Q 10 8 3
                    ◇ A K 8 5 3
                    ♣ A Q 10 7
```

It would have been wiser, with his top-heavy hand, to rebid two spades over two clubs. However, we have some chances in five clubs.

Having held the first trick with the king of hearts, West makes the obvious switch to a trump. That rules out a cross-ruff, which at best now would produce seven tricks in trumps and three in diamonds. And playing on the diamond suit won't produce eleven tricks either, unless by some miracle a defender holds J 10 9 alone.

What about dummy's spades? I think there may be chances if I can bring down the ace in two or three rounds. Suppose I win the club lead in dummy, ruff a spade, play a diamond to the queen, and ruff a spade high. Then, if the ace of spades has not appeared, I can draw trumps with dummy's K J and play another spade, hoping for a 3–3 break.

That seems the best plan, so I put in the 9 of clubs at trick two and lead a spade. Without a flicker, East produces the ace.

East must know I have not got the queen of spades, so I have to assume that the spades are 5 – 1. If that is so, I cannot bring in the suit and must play for some tricks in diamonds. After ruffing the spade with the queen of clubs I play a diamond to the queen and return a club to the 10. That leaves:

♠ K 10 7 6 5 3
♡ —
◇ —
♣ K J

♠ —
♡ Q 10 8
◇ A K 8 5
♣ A

All follow to the ace and king of diamonds. On the fourth round West discards a spade and dummy ruffs. There is no point in drawing the last trump, so I play the king of spades from dummy. East pounces on this with his remaining trump. That puts me back in the game, I think. Instead of overruffing, I discard a heart, and East, slightly taken aback, exits with a low heart. When the 10 fetches the ace I make the rest of the tricks, as my queen of hearts and 8 of diamonds are both winners and I still have a trump. The full hand was:

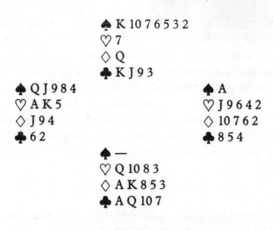

Post-mortem

This was perhaps a hand for the defence more than for the declarer. Observe the trap into which East fell at the finish:

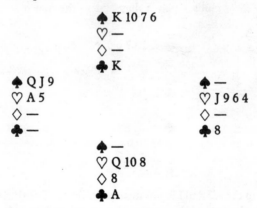

When East ruffed the king of spades he was saving one trick (the king of spades) but was giving away two (the queen of hearts and an extra trump in effect). If East discards on the king of spades declarer can make only two more tricks—either a trump and a diamond or two trumps.

The lesson for declarer is that, in a position like this where trumps are scarce, it is often a sound move to let an opponent ruff with a losing trump. The trick comes back at once, because declarer can now make his trumps separately and also cash the side winner; and if the defender has to make a disadvantageous lead after ruffing, the trick comes back with interest.

32. Not Against Garozzo

Bridge in the Canary Islands, like the climate, is more relaxed than in some of the Continental tournaments. It is, perhaps, more difficult to keep one's game up to standard. Playing in the pairs at Las Palmas one year, I hold in third position:

♠ A 7 6 4   ♡ 8   ◇ 10 7 6 5   ♣ A 10 6 3

My partner deals and opens **one heart.** I respond **one spade** and he raises to **three spades.** He must have four spades for the double raise, so I reject any thought of three notrumps and bid four spades, concluding an uneventful auction.

South	West	North	East
—	—	1♡	pass
1♠	pass	3♠	pass
4♠	pass	pass	pass

West leads the queen of diamonds and I see that partner's hand, like mine, is on the low side for his bidding:

♠ K J 9 3
♡ A Q 10 5 2
◇ A 4
♣ J 9

◇ Q led

♠ A 7 6 4
♡ 8
◇ 10 7 6 5
♣ A 10 6 3

There is a loser in each minor suit and plenty of work to do. I am not sure how the hand will develop, but the natural way to begin is to put on the ace of diamonds and lead the jack of clubs. East covers with the king and I return a low club to the 9. East takes this with the queen and plays king of diamonds, followed by a low diamond, which is ruffed in dummy.

I am not proposing to take the heart finesse, so I continue with ace of hearts and a heart ruff, followed by the 10 of clubs. West looks at this for some moments, then discards the king of hearts. After this trick the position is:

♠ K J 9
♡ Q 10
◇ —
♣ —

♠ A 7 6
♡ —
◇ 10
♣ 6

It should be possible to count the hand now. West began with a doubleton club and four diamonds (he led the queen and the jack is still out). I'm not playing against Garozzo, so I'm disposed to regard the king of hearts as a true card from an original holding of K x x. In that case West has four trumps.

My first thought is to play ace of spades, then finesse the jack of spades and play the 10 of hearts, ruffing with my last trump. That's no good; if West began with ♠ Q 10 x x he will overruff and lead the jack of diamonds, establishing a second trump trick.

Then what about ace of spades, jack of spades, queen of hearts? No, West will ruff and exit with a trump, leaving the 10 of hearts a loser.

As I cannot make a certainty of the contract by leading trumps, I play my last club. West discards a diamond and dummy ruffs with the 9. Now I could ruff a heart with the ace of spades and finesse the jack (to exit with a diamond is the same thing), losing only if East's singleton spade is the queen. Just in time I see an improvement: cash the king of spades, ruff with the ace, and make the jack *en passant*. As it happens, the queen falls under the King. I lose one trump trick, but that is all, the full hand being:

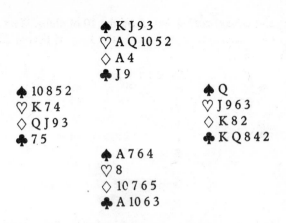

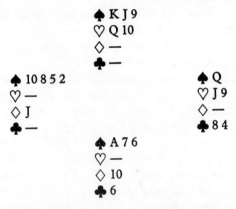

Post-mortem

The position round the table at the finish was:

Note that to play the ace of spades first is not good enough, even though the queen falls. (The situation is the same as when I envisaged finessing the jack on the second round.)

After the club has been ruffed, the king of spades is an unusual safety play. It still wins, of course, if West's spades are Q 10 x x; after a heart has been ruffed with the ace of spades, a diamond from hand at trick 12 establishes a trick for the jack of spades.

I think we must all have missed this form of play on occasions. Consider this ending:

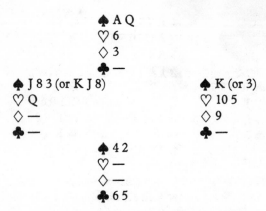

Playing in a spade contract, with the lead in dummy, South knows that the trumps are 3 – 1 and that he can safely ruff a heart. The ace of spades first guarantees three tricks whether East's singleton is the king or a low card.

33. Lonely on a Rock

Playing in a popular pairs event against unfamiliar opponents, I hold in third position:

♠ A Q J 9 3   ♡ Q 8 7   ◇ 9 7 4 2   ♣ 5

With neither side vulnerable, my partner opens **one club.** I respond **one spade** and West, on my left, comes in with **two diamonds,** which is passed round to me. I have promising defence against diamonds, and if they were vulnerable I would certainly double, for a likely 200. As it is, we would need to get them two down to beat a part score our way. Not very courageously, I bid **two spades.** My partner now bids **three diamonds,** their suit. Presumably he is prepared to play either in three spades or, if I can bid it, three notrumps. With my four diamonds, there is a danger of a ruff if we play in spades, so I bid **three notrumps,** not very happily. The bidding ends there:

South	West	North	East
—	—	1♣	pass
1♠	2◇	pass	pass
2♠	pass	3◇	pass
3NT	pass	pass	pass

West leads the king of diamonds and the first thing I see is that we have no guard in this suit:

```
              ♠ K 10
              ♡ A J 3
              ◇ J 8 6
              ♣ A Q 9 6 4

◇ K led

              ♠ A Q J 9 3
              ♡ Q 8 7
              ◇ 9 7 4 2
              ♣ 5
```

Perhaps East will have the 10 of diamonds and block the suit? No, he follows with the 3. Unexpectedly, he follows to the next round of diamonds also. So West has overcalled at the two level on a four-card suit! We would have murdered them in two diamonds doubled. What was I thinking about?

West plays off two more diamond winners, dummy discarding a club, East the 9 and 4 of hearts. West then switches to the 5 of hearts. I don't believe they are both playing a deep deceptive game, so I go up with the ace, on which East drops the 6.

Even if the club finesse is right, as I imagine it is, I have only eight tricks. If East held five clubs and the king of hearts there would be a straightforward squeeze, but against the present opposition I have a better plan. Suppose I finesse the queen of clubs, then leave the A 9 on the table as an imaginary threat: there is a good chance that they will both keep clubs and unguard the hearts.

I overtake the king of spades with the ace and finesse the queen of clubs, which holds. Then, leaving the ace of clubs lonely on a rock, I run three more spade tricks, reducing to:

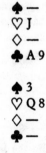

♠ —
♡ J
♢ —
♣ A 9

♠ 3
♡ Q 8
♢ —
♣ —

West has discarded one club and one heart, East has followed suit. On the last spade West discards the 10 of hearts, dummy the jack, and East, with an anxious look at his partner, the king. My Q 8 of hearts take the last two tricks, the full hand being:

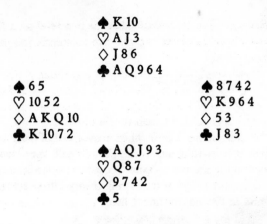

```
              ♠ K 10
              ♡ A J 3
              ◇ J 8 6
              ♣ A Q 9 6 4
♠ 6 5                        ♠ 8 7 4 2
♡ 10 5 2                     ♡ K 9 6 4
◇ A K Q 10                   ◇ 5 3
♣ K 10 7 2                   ♣ J 8 3
              ♠ A Q J 9 3
              ♡ Q 8 7
              ◇ 9 7 4 2
              ♣ 5
```

Post-mortem

This was the position round the table when West had to make his second discard:

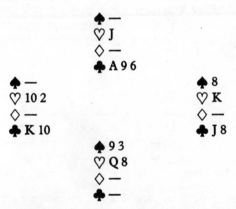

```
              ♠ —
              ♡ J
              ◇ —
              ♣ A 9 6
♠ —                          ♠ 8
♡ 10 2                       ♡ K
◇ —                          ◇ —
♣ K 10                       ♣ J 8
              ♠ 9 3
              ♡ Q 8
              ◇ —
              ♣ —
```

Seeing the clubs in dummy, and placing his partner with the king of hearts, it was not unnatural that West should let go hearts. Similarly, on the last spade, East was deceived into thinking that he must keep the clubs and trust his partner for the queen of hearts.

This type of pseudo-squeeze is quite easy to foresee and execute. The essential element in the plan is to leave a master card abandoned on the table. There is always a good chance that one or both defenders will assume that it is necessary to protect this suit and will present declarer with unexpected winners in another suit.

34. A Small Stratagem

Sometimes at rubber bridge I wish the "unusual notrump" had never been born. Players either use it when they shouldn't or, when two notrumps would be natural and is the obvious call, they won't bid it.

My partner on the present occasion is a lady who reads all the books but is not always successful at translating theory into practice. We are vulnerable and in second position I hold:

♠ 8 4 3　♡ K 7 4 2　♢ 5 3　♣ Q 9 7 3

East, on my right, opens **one spade** and after two passes my partner **doubles.** East now jumps to **three spades.** That is too high for me, but when it comes round to my partner she doubles **again,** presumably for take-out. I bid **four hearts,** which is briskly doubled on my left. Partner now produces a mysterious **four notrumps.** East doubles and I bid **five clubs.** West **doubles** again and all pass. It has been an alarming auction:

South	West	North	East
—	—	—	1♠
pass	pass	double	3♠
pass	pass	double	pass
4♡	double	4NT	double
5♣	double	pass	pass
pass			

West leads the 5 of hearts and I await my partner's hand with interest.

　　　　　　　　♠ Q 10 9 5
　　　　　　　　♡ A J 10
　　　　　　　　♢ A Q
　　　　　　　　♣ A K 10 4

♡ 5 led

　　　　　　　　♠ 8 4 3
　　　　　　　　♡ K 7 4 2
　　　　　　　　♢ 5 3
　　　　　　　　♣ Q 9 7 3

Five clubs! What a contract to reach!

At least the opening lead is not unfavourable. The 10 of hearts holds the first trick, East playing the 8, doubtless a singleton. West is obviously void in spades and probably has four trumps.

I don't see anything better than to draw trumps and set up a spade trick. On the ace of clubs East drops the 8. That gives me an extra entry to hand, because now I can pick up the jack of clubs without abandoning the lead in trumps. To do this, I play the 10 of clubs to the queen, East discarding a spade. West covers the 7 of clubs with the jack, but I am able to return to the 9 and finesse the jack of hearts, on which East discards a diamond. After the ace of hearts has been cashed the position is:

♠ Q 10 9 5
♡ —
◇ A Q
♣ —

♠ 8 4 3
♡ K
◇ 5 3
♣ —

East has made five discards—two spades and three diamonds, if I remember correctly. In that case he is down to ♠ A K J x and ◇ K 10.

What happens if I lead a spade from dummy? East will take his winners and exit with a fourth spade. A diamond can't be worse. In fact . . . Well, let's see.

When I play ace and queen of diamonds East wins and leads the ace of spades. He is looking quite cheerful, because he intends to follow with a low spade, retaining the K J over dummy's Q 10. But on the ace of spades I unblock with a 10 for the second time. When East follows with a low spade I am able to win with the 8 and enjoy a trick with the king of hearts. One down! Not bad when you look at the four hands:

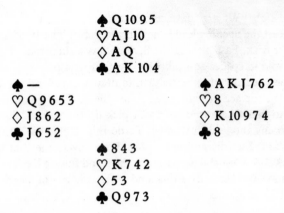

♠ Q 10 9 5
♥ A J 10
♦ A Q
♣ A K 10 4

♠ —
♥ Q 9 6 5 3
♦ J 8 6 2
♣ J 6 5 2

♠ A K J 7 6 2
♥ 8
♦ K 10 9 7 4
♣ 8

♠ 8 4 3
♥ K 7 4 2
♦ 5 3
♣ Q 9 7 3

"I might have made four notrumps," said my partner—a little ungratefully, I thought.

"I don't know about four notrumps," I said. "You might have made three, certainly. Why didn't you bid a straightforward two notrumps on the first round, instead of doubling?"

"I thought two notrumps would be something special," she said vaguely.

Two notrumps in the protective position is often based on a good minor suit, it is true, but it is natural by definition. I tried again:

"Your double of three spades was for take-out, you know. Did you think of bidding three notrumps at that point?"

"I thought you would take that for the unusual notrump."

She wouldn't bid two notrumps or three notrumps when she had the chance, but expects me to pass four notrumps! Oh well, it's not worth pursuing.

Post-mortem

The defenders also were displeased with one another. East complained of the opening lead, pointing out that a diamond would probably have led to 800. West then suggested that East would have done better in the end game to keep ♠ A K J and ♦ K 10 x instead of four spades and two diamonds. True, against that defence I must lose four of the last six tricks. East thought he had the situation under control as it was; he overlooked my small stratagem with the 10 of spades.

35. The Jig-Saw

We all, at times, make assumptions about the lie of a particular suit; the next step is to consider what follows, in other suits, from that assumption.

Playing in a team-of-four match against strong opponents, I hold in second position:

♠ K 10 9 7   ♡ 8 6   ◇ A 9 4   ♣ 9 6 5 2

We are vulnerable, they are not. East, on my right, opens **one heart**, I pass, and West bids **two diamonds**, which my partner **doubles**. East jumps to **three hearts** and I feel entitled to come in with **three spades**. West passes and North raises to **four spades**, the final bid.

South	West	North	East
—	—	—	1♡
pass	2◇	double	3♡
3♠	pass	4♠	pass
pass	pass		

West leads the 2 of hearts and I see that we have bid a very thin game when this dummy goes down:

```
              ♠ A J 8 4 2
              ♡ 5
              ◇ 8 7 2
              ♣ A Q 10 7
♡ 2 led
              ♠ K 10 9 7
              ♡ 8 6
              ◇ A 9 4
              ♣ 9 6 5 2
```

East wins the first trick with the king of hearts and returns the jack of diamonds. This could be a singleton, so I go up with the ace and ruff the second heart, West playing the 10. Now, how am I going to play the trumps? It is not just a question of how *do* they lie, but of how I *want* them to lie.

East must hold the king of clubs for his bidding and my best hope for the contract is to find him with a doubleton king. I have already played him for a singleton diamond, and if he has K x of clubs I may be able to throw him in on the second round of clubs and obtain a ruff-and-discard.

As West did not support the hearts, East must hold seven, together with one diamond and, I am assuming, two clubs. In that case he will hold three spades.

It cannot be wrong, before I leave the dummy, to cash the ace of clubs. Then comes ace of spades, followed by a low spade to the 10, which holds. After the king of spades has drawn the outstanding trump the position is:

♠ 8
♡ —
◇ 8 7
♣ Q 10 7

♠ 9
♡ —
◇ 9 4
♣ 9 6 5

I lead a low club and when West plays low I put in the 10, fairly confident that East will win with the king and give me a ruff-and-discard. The full hand was:

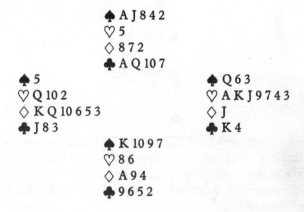

		♠ A J 8 4 2		
		♡ 5		
		◇ 8 7 2		
		♣ A Q 10 7		
♠ 5				♠ Q 6 3
♡ Q 10 2				♡ A K J 9 7 4 3
◇ K Q 10 6 5 3				◇ J
♣ J 8 3				♣ K 4
		♠ K 10 9 7		
		♡ 8 6		
		◇ A 9 4		
		♣ 9 6 5 2		

The decision to play East for Q x x of trumps was a good example of "second-degree assumption". Declarer has placed East with seven hearts and one diamond and can make the contract only if East has a K x of clubs and can be end-played. Therefore it must be assumed that East has three spades.

Here is another hand on the same theme, which was found interesting when first published:

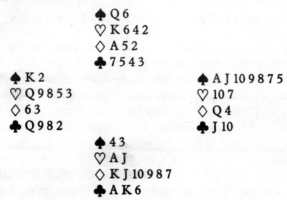

```
                    ♠ Q 6
                    ♡ K 6 4 2
                    ◇ A 5 2
                    ♣ 7 5 4 3
   ♠ K 2                          ♠ A J 10 9 8 7 5
   ♡ Q 9 8 5 3                    ♡ 10 7
   ◇ 6 3                          ◇ Q 4
   ♣ Q 9 8 2                      ♣ J 10
                    ♠ 4 3
                    ♡ A J
                    ◇ K J 10 9 8 7
                    ♣ A K 6
```

North – South were vulnerable and the bidding went:

South	West	North	East
—	pass	pass	3♠
4◇	pass	5◇	pass
pass	pass		

The defenders made two tricks in spades, then switched to a club. South won, cashed the king of diamonds, then ran the jack, losing to East's queen. This was one down, but declarer made the rest of the tricks by squeezing West in hearts and clubs.

South realised that if he had played for the drop in diamonds he would have made the contract by way of the same squeeze. "I had to play for the odds," he remarked. "East was likely to be short in diamonds."

This was true so far as it went, but it wasn't the answer. If East has a singleton diamond, how can South make the contract? The squeeze was possible only because West had exclusive control of hearts and clubs. If East has a singleton diamond he must hold three cards in either hearts or clubs and the squeeze won't work.

Every hand is a jig-saw puzzle and every piece must fit.

36. Welcome Stranger

Playing in the open pairs at Juan-Les-Pins, I pick up a hand that would be a welcome stranger at rubber bridge:

♠ A K Q J 2 ♡ — ◇ A K 9 3 ♣ A K Q 4

Opponents are vulnerable, we are not. I open **two clubs,** but we are not destined to enjoy an easy passage, for West overcalls with **three hearts.** My partner passes, and so does East.

There are three possibilities now—double, three spades, and four hearts. Most players, if the same sequence occurs at other tables, will choose four hearts, but it seems to me there is a disadvantage in that: if partner responds with a forced bid of five clubs or five diamonds, how high do you go? That's the trouble with very big hands—you can't expect to get much co-operation. On the whole, I prefer a simple **three spades.** If partner makes an anti-system pass, I shall have something to hold over him for the rest of the week; but if he volunteers a minor suit I shall know we are close to a grand slam.

Over three spades partner summons up **four spades.** It is not easy to find out whether he has the right cards for seven, so I settle for **six spades.** Most pairs, I am sure, will have a more scientific auction than ours:

South	West	North	East
2♣	3♡	pass	pass
3♠	pass	4♠	pass
6♠	pass	pass	pass

West leads the ace of hearts and I see that we are quite high enough:

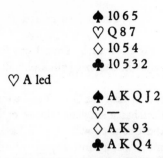

♡ A led

♠ A K Q J 2
♡ —
◇ A K 9 3
♣ A K Q 4

If there had been no adverse bidding, the natural way to set about this contract would be to play off ace, king and another diamond, planning to ruff the fourth round if necessary. However, in view of West's vulnerable pre-empt, bad breaks must be expected in at least one minor suit. Another point is that, according to their convention card, the opponents lead king from ace-king. If West has not departed from convention, then there is a good chance that East may have K x and that I can set up the queen as a trick. I ruff the ace with a high trump, therefore, and take three rounds of spades, finishing in dummy. West surprisingly follows suit and East discards the 2 of diamonds. I play a heart from dummy, the king appears, and I ruff with my last trump.

As West is already marked with eleven cards in the majors, I am not hopeful of a 3 – 2 club break. West follows to the first round but discards on the second. These are the remaining cards:

East still has the J 9 of clubs and four diamonds. If I can get to dummy to make the queen of hearts I will have enough tricks, but how am I going to do that?

West may have a plain singleton in diamonds or he may have a singleton honour. Suppose I lead the ace of diamonds and the queen or jack falls; I can follow with the 9, and if East refuses to win I can end-play him.

But suppose West's diamond is a low card. Then I can follow with the 9, but East, with Q J 8 7, will win and exit with an honour, leaving me in hand.

What about leading the 9 first? If East has Q J 8 7 and wins the trick he will be on play. And if West has a singleton queen or jack? Ah! He will have to lead a heart and this trick will squeeze East.

So far as I can see, the 9 must win against any distribution. West in practice plays a low diamond, East wins with the queen and returns the 8. This runs to dummy's 10 and my losing club goes away on the queen of hearts. The full hand was:

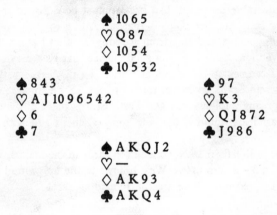

Pairs who reached a slam in clubs were out of luck. After a heart lead, and a second heart later, the defenders must make at least two tricks.

Post-mortem

This was the position after seven tricks:

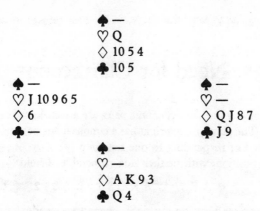

♠ —
♡ Q
◇ 10 5 4
♣ 10 5

♠ —
♡ J 10 9 6 5
◇ 6
♣ —

♠ —
♡ —
◇ Q J 8 7
♣ J 9

♠ —
♡ —
◇ A K 9 3
♣ Q 4

Now the 9 of diamonds ensures the contract. If West has a singleton queen or jack he must win and exit with a heart, which will squeeze his partner.

37. Need for Clarification

My opponents in the *Sunday Times* pairs are a well-known American partnership. The player on my right has a famous name not unconnected with a method of responding to one notrump.

In fourth position, with neither side vulnerable, I hold:

♠ A K 7   ♡ A K Q 8 6   ◇ A 8 4 2   ♣ 6

After two passes East, on my right, opens **two spades,** a weak two bid. My partner and I play the same conventions over a weak two as over a one bid, so I **double** for take-out. West passes and partner bids **three clubs.** I have a choice now between three hearts and three notrumps. Three notrumps seems the better proposition; the fact that I have not mentioned my good heart suit may turn out to my advantage. West **doubles,** which is a little ominous. I am not going to run, so there the bidding ends.

South	West	North	East
—	pass	pass	2♠
double	pass	3♣	pass
3NT	double	pass	pass
pass			

West leads the jack of hearts and, as expected, partner has little to contribute:

♠ Q 6 2
♡ 5 3
◇ 10 6
♣ J 8 7 5 4 2

♡ J led

♠ A K 7
♡ A K Q 8 6
◇ A 8 4 2
♣ 6

West can have a singleton spade at most, so no doubt the opening lead is from length. By ducking I may gain a tempo, perhaps even a trick. This possibility is increased when East plays the 7. I drop the 8, hoping that West, missing the 6, will construe the 7 as encouragement.

After some sighs and precautionary mutterings (designed to show that he suspects the trap) West follows with a low heart. This runs to my 6, East discarding a spade. I play off ace, king and queen of hearts, discarding two clubs and a spade from the table. East throws a second spade, then a diamond, and finally the 9 of clubs.

East evidently has six spades and is nervous of throwing another in case I hold A K x x. Whether he is 4 – 2 or 3 – 3 in the minors I can't be sure; 4 – 2 is more likely, because I imagine that West's double was based on a strong holding in clubs.

Anyway, there is nothing to do but hope I can establish a second trick in diamonds. I lead a low diamond and West plays the jack, which holds the trick. West exits with a low club, East producing the ace. This is the position, with East on lead:

$$\spadesuit \text{Q 6}$$
$$\heartsuit \text{—}$$
$$\diamondsuit \text{10}$$
$$\clubsuit \text{J 8 7}$$

$$\spadesuit \text{A K 7}$$
$$\heartsuit \text{—}$$
$$\diamondsuit \text{A 8 4}$$
$$\clubsuit \text{—}$$

The jack of spades from East runs to dummy's queen, West following suit. East has only two diamonds left, and if they include the king I am going to make the contract. When I lead the 10 of diamonds from dummy, East plays low. I go up with the ace, cash the ace of spades, and exit with a low diamond. East has to win and I make the last two tricks with the king of spades and the 8 of diamonds. The full hand was:

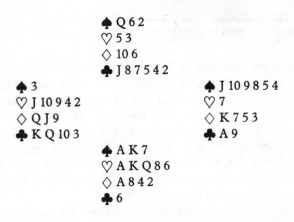

```
          ♠ Q 6 2
          ♡ 5 3
          ◇ 10 6
          ♣ J 8 7 5 4 2
♠ 3                           ♠ J 10 9 8 5 4
♡ J 10 9 4 2                  ♡ 7
◇ Q J 9                       ◇ K 7 5 3
♣ K Q 10 3                    ♣ A 9
          ♠ A K 7
          ♡ A K Q 8 6
          ◇ A 8 4 2
          ♣ 6
```

Post-mortem

Declarer's eighth trick came when West led a low heart at trick two, and the ninth when he was able to establish a long diamond after East had discarded a diamond. The defence could not recover after West had won the first trick in diamonds. The position at that stage was:

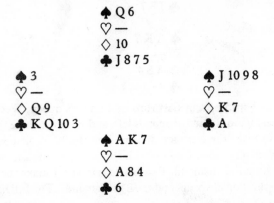

```
          ♠ Q 6
          ♡ —
          ◇ 10
          ♣ J 8 7 5
♠ 3                   ♠ J 10 9 8
♡ —                   ♡ —
◇ Q 9                 ◇ K 7
♣ K Q 10 3            ♣ A
          ♠ A K 7
          ♡ —
          ◇ A 8 4
          ♣ 6
```

The clubs were blocked, and an extra trick in diamonds could always be developed without letting West into the lead; if East goes up with the king on the second round he is allowed to hold the trick.

East could have beaten the contract earlier by overtaking the jack of diamonds with the king and cashing the ace of clubs. The defence would have been easier from his side if West had led his singleton spade at any point, to clarify the position in that suit. This is a point worth bearing in mind when partner has shown a long suit. If you don't lead it, he will wonder whether you are void, have a singleton honour, or what. Unless there is a very good alternative, it is better to lead his suit.

38. With an Innocent Air

Playing in the final of the Two Stars at the Eastbourne Congress, I hold in second position:

♠ 5 4　♡ A K Q 10 4　♢ K 8　♣ Q 9 6 2

Both sides are vulnerable and after a pass on my right I open **one heart.** West passes and my partner responds **two diamonds.** I rebid **two hearts** and he raises to **four hearts,** which all pass.

South	West	North	East
—	—	—	pass
1♡	pass	2♢	pass
2♡	pass	4♡	pass
pass	pass		

West leads the 6 of spades and partner goes down with:

　　　　　　♠ K 10 3
　　　　　　♡ 8 6 2
　　　　　　♢ A Q 7 6 2
　　　　　　♣ A 8

♠ 6 led

　　　　　　♠ 5 4
　　　　　　♡ A K Q 10 4
　　　　　　♢ K 8
　　　　　　♣ Q 9 6 2

There is no reason to suppose that West has underled an ace, so I play low from dummy. East puts on the 9 and without much thought returns a low trump. I was expecting a club switch to attack dummy's entry. On the ace of hearts West drops the jack, and when I follow with two more hearts he discards the 5 and 4 of clubs. On the 10 of hearts West plays the 3 of clubs and I have to discard from dummy, the position being:

♠ K 10
♡ —
◊ A Q 7 6 2
♣ A 8

♠ 5
♡ 4
◊ K 8
♣ Q 9 6 2

The contract is not in danger: I have nine top tricks and can set up a long diamond unless they are 5 – 1, which is unlikely. However, I am sure they are not 3 – 3, because in that case East would have been afraid of discards and would have given serious thought to cashing the ace of spades at trick two.

Obviously I am not going to throw a diamond from dummy. I could discard a spade, but by the time I have ruffed the fourth round of diamonds I won't have any trumps left and will make just the ace of clubs and the long diamond. I think I retain more options if I keep the K 10 of spades and throw a club from the table.

All follow to the king and ace of diamonds. I discard a club on the queen, and so does West. We are now down to:

♠ K 10
♡ —
◊ 7 6
♣ A

♠ 5
♡ 4
◊ —
♣ Q 9 6

On the 6 of diamonds East plays the jack. Now it's a free shot to discard the 5 of spades, a loser on loser. Sure enough, when East is allowed to hold the jack of diamonds he leads a low spade with an innocent air. I let this run to the king and make what I trust will be a valuable overtrick, the full hand being:

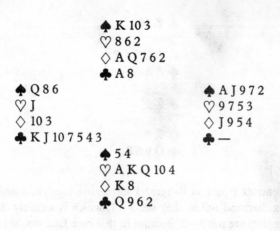

```
              ♠ K 10 3
              ♡ 8 6 2
              ◇ A Q 7 6 2
              ♣ A 8
♠ Q 8 6                        ♠ A J 9 7 2
♡ J                            ♡ 9 7 5 3
◇ 10 3                         ◇ J 9 5 4
♣ K J 10 7 5 4 3               ♣ —
              ♠ 5 4
              ♡ A K Q 10 4
              ◇ K 8
              ♣ Q 9 6 2
```

Post-mortem

This was the position round the table when the fourth diamond was led:

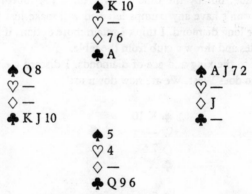

```
              ♠ K 10
              ♡ —
              ◇ 7 6
              ♣ A
♠ Q 8                          ♠ A J 7 2
♡ —                            ♡ —
◇ —                            ◇ J
♣ K J 10                       ♣ —
              ♠ 5
              ♡ 4
              ◇ —
              ♣ Q 9 6
```

South discards a spade and East is left on play. The loser-on-loser gains only because East cannot exit in clubs, but it cannot cost a trick and there were, as a matter of fact, indications that East might be void of clubs. (West had discarded four and East's failure to lead a club at trick two was significant.)

The other important play was the discard of a club from dummy on the fourth heart. It looks fairly natural to discard a spade and retain the possibility of setting up a second club trick by playing ace and another; but declarer should foresee that if he is going to use his last trump to ruff a diamond he will run out of steam and will never enjoy a trick with the queen of clubs.

126

39. Feat of Circumnavigation

Most textbooks contain an example of the *Devil's Coup*, where the declarer, with an original trump holding of A 9 x opposite K 10 x x x, contrives in the end game to avoid losing a trick although one defender has Q x and the other J x x. There are other combinations where the same kind of play is occasionally possible.

In a team-of-four match neither side is vulnerable and I hold in fourth position:

♠ K 9 7 6 4 2   ♡ K 9 6 3   ◇ Q 10   ♣ 4

After a pass by the dealer my partner opens **one notrump** and the next player passes. We are playing the Precision system, in which one notrump is 13 – 15 in all positions. My hand is not easy to value, because much will depend on the fit. Eventually I decide in favour of **three spades,** not forcing, as we play it, but inviting game in the suit. Partner gives me **four spades** and all pass.

South	West	North	East
—	pass	1NT	pass
3♠	pass	4♠	pass
pass	pass		

West leads the king of clubs and partner puts down:

♠ Q 8
♡ A Q J
◇ K J 8 5
♣ J 9 6 2

♣ K led

♠ K 9 7 6 4 2
♡ K 9 6 3
◇ Q 10
♣ 4

This is not at all promising, with two minor suit aces to lose and A J 10 of trumps against me. Perhaps I overestimated my 6 – 4 – 2 – 1 hand.

East plays the 8 of clubs on the first trick and West continues with the 3 of clubs. The 9 is headed by the ace and I ruff.

It looks as though I need to find West with A x of trumps, or either defender with a doubleton J 10. As a first move, I think I'll force out the ace of diamonds. There is no great danger and I may learn a little more about the hand. West takes the queen with the ace and switches to a heart.

The chance of finding West with A x of trumps is now non-existent, because he passed originally and has turned up with ace of diamonds and K Q 10 x of clubs. It is possible, in theory, with a trump holding of Q 8 opposite K 9 7, to circumnavigate A J x or A 10 x in the East hand. Let's move cautiously in that direction.

I have to reduce my trumps, so I ruff a club, enter dummy with a heart, cash the king of diamonds, and ruff another club, to which all follow. This leaves:

♠ Q 8
♡ Q
◇ J 8
♣ —

♠ K 9 7
♡ K 9
◇ —
♣ —

My impression, from the fall of the cards, is that all the suits are breaking evenly. A heart to the queen stands up and my fourth heart is discarded on the jack of diamonds. When the 8 of diamonds is led from the table, East looks worried. Eventually he ruffs with the jack. I overruff and finesse the 8 on the way back. This forces the ace, so I lose only one trump trick, the full hand being:

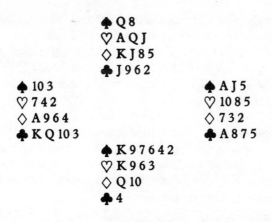

```
                    ♠ Q 8
                    ♡ A Q J
                    ◇ K J 8 5
                    ♣ J 9 6 2
    ♠ 10 3                          ♠ A J 5
    ♡ 7 4 2                         ♡ 10 8 5
    ◇ A 9 6 4                       ◇ 7 3 2
    ♣ K Q 10 3                      ♣ A 8 7 5
                    ♠ K 9 7 6 4 2
                    ♡ K 9 6 3
                    ◇ Q 10
                    ♣ 4
```

Post-mortem

This was the position round the table at the finish:

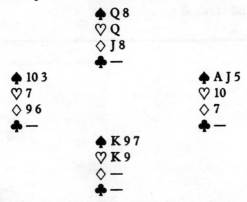

```
                    ♠ Q 8
                    ♡ Q
                    ◇ J 8
                    ♣ —
    ♠ 10 3                          ♠ A J 5
    ♡ 7                             ♡ 10
    ◇ 9 6                           ◇ 7
    ♣ —                             ♣ —
                    ♠ K 9 7
                    ♡ K 9
                    ◇ —
                    ♣ —
```

Declarer played a heart to the queen, cashed the jack of diamonds, and led a fourth diamond, robbing the defence of an expected trump trick.

The *Devil's Coup* is seldom accomplished at the table, because the distribution of the defending hands has to be exactly right, as it was here. However, there are times when a frontal assault on the trump suit is bound to fail, and on these occasions the *coup* is worth trying. Observe this ending:

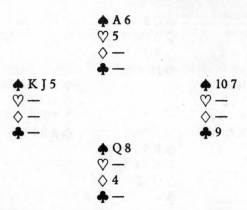

Spades are trumps, the lead is in dummy, and West is marked with the king of spades. An ordinary *coup-en-passant* (ace of spades, followed by 5 of hearts) cannot win, but the 5 of hearts from dummy holds the defenders to one trick, however they play.

40. Fate Worse Than Death

"I have a hard luck story for you," said a friend at the club. "To begin with, I was playing with so-and-so." He named the worst player in the club, one who is incapable of playing the simplest dummy.

"Don't tell me," I said. "I was playing with him the other day and . . ."

"Let me tell my story first," said the Ancient Mariner firmly. "We were vulnerable, I was third to speak, and I picked up this hand:

♠ A J 10 8 6 3 2　♡ —　♢ A 4　♣ A 7 4 2

"I will give you a small test. What is the worst that could happen in the present circumstances?"

"He opened four hearts," I said, making the obvious suggestion.

"Worse than that. He opened **one spade**."

"That's bad," I agreed. "Still, you don't have to bid seven. Even he could make six, surely?"

"Yes, that's what I thought. I bid **six spades** and he went to **seven spades** because, he said, he needed a grand slam to get him out on the afternoon."

South	West	North	East
1♠	pass	6♠	pass
7♠	pass	pass	pass

"The queen of diamonds was led and these were the two hands:

　　　　　　　♠ A J 10 8 6 3 2
　　　　　　　♡ —
　　　　　　　♢ A 4
　　　　　　　♣ A 7 4 2

♢ Q led

　　　　　　　♠ K Q 9 5
　　　　　　　♡ A K 7
　　　　　　　♢ 8 7
　　　　　　　♣ K 9 8 3

"Of course it didn't occur to him to throw two clubs on the hearts and ruff out a club for his thirteenth trick. He discarded a diamond

131

and a club on the top hearts, fiddled around, and finally gave up a club."

"You knew he'd muddle it one way or another," I said. "Did you think of transferring to seven notrumps?"

"I might have done that, I suppose. But I don't think I would have had much chance. The full hand was something like this:

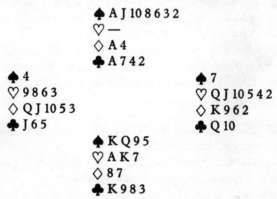

"As you can see, the red suits were guarded on both sides; not much chance of a squeeze."

"You have got a guard-finesse position in clubs, though", I pointed out. "You can do funny things with guard squeezes, even when the other suits are well protected. You would be playing as North, so the lead would be a heart from East. Let's try the effect of cashing the top hearts and playing off a number of spades, unblocking the clubs in dummy."

We ticked off the cards, arriving at this position:

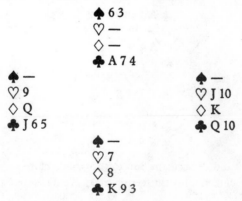

On the next spade East cannot let go a club, because this exposes his partner to a finesse against the jack. East's natural discard is a heart. South unblocks in clubs again, throwing the 9. West's 9 of hearts and queen of diamonds have the same value now. Say he chooses to throw the 9 of hearts.

On the last spade East must keep his jack of hearts, as his partner has unguarded this suit. He must discard the king of diamonds. South now throws his 7 of hearts and West is squeezed.

Post-mortem

Guard squeezes, as I remarked above, are funny things. As a rule, a menace card which is controlled by both opponents is useless in a squeeze ending. Here both the 7 of hearts and the 8 of diamonds are covered on both sides, yet there is no defence to the squeeze.

As for the bidding, I must admit that with weak partners I generally aim to play the slam hands, even if it means a rather dangerous transfer from his suit into notrumps. So often, a little extra in technique or deception will be worth a trick.

The worst way to hog the bidding is to rush into three notrumps whenever you hold twelve points and partner has opened the bidding. Apart from the silly result you will sometimes get, partner will see what you are doing and will play worse than ever. On the other hand, certain tactical procedures are very sensible. For example, with ♠ K 10 x x ♡ A J x ◇ x ♣ A Q 10 x x, open one spade if your partner is a bad player of the dummy. If he supports spades you will be playing it, and if he responds two diamonds you can rebid two notrumps.

41. A Minor Ambition

The so-called "Michaels cue-bids" are undoubtedly one of the best of the modern conventions. In place of the ponderous cue-bids of the Culbertson era, immediate overcalls in the opponent's suit denote various types of distributional hand, usually below the strength of a take-out double.

Playing in a pairs event against a husband-and-wife partnership, I am fourth to speak and hold:

♠ J 9 4   ♡ Q 10 4   ◇ K 10 6 5 2   ♣ 9 5

With both sides vulnerable, the opponent on my left opens **one diamond** and my partner overcalls with **two diamonds**. This suggests initially a limited hand with at least 5 – 4 in the majors. After a pass by the next player I respond **two hearts**. The opener bids **three clubs** and my partner contests with **three hearts,** which is passed out. The bidding has been:

South	West	North	East
—	1◇	2◇	pass
2♡	3♣	3♡	pass
pass	pass		

It is unusual for a Michaels overcaller to bid again freely, so I am expecting a fair dummy. After the lead of the king of spades my partner puts down:

♠ Q 10 5 3
♡ K 8 6 5 2
◇ —
♣ A Q 6 3

♠ K led

♠ J 9 4
♡ Q 10 4
◇ K 10 6 5 2
♣ 9 5

East plays the 2 of spades on the opening lead and West switches to the jack of clubs. Dummy's queen holds, East dropping the 7. I lead the 2 of hearts from dummy and East plays the 3.

As the spades appear to be 3 – 3 (since the opponents did not play for a ruff) and West has bid two suits, it seems very likely that the trumps will be 5 – 0. To win the first round of trumps with a finesse of the 4 has long been one of my minor ambitions, and this seems to be the moment. I insert the 4 of hearts, therefore, and it holds the trick, West discarding a club.

Pleased with that success, I ruff a diamond and lead the 3 of spades, to clear my spade trick. West wins with the ace and leads the king of clubs to dummy's ace, East completing an echo.

After cashing the queen of spades I lead a club from dummy. East discards a diamond and I ruff with the 10. Things are going well:

♠ 10
♡ K 8 6
◇ —
♣ 6

♠ —
♡ Q
◇ K 8 6 5
♣ —

Another diamond ruff stands up and then I lead a fourth club from dummy. East, I know, is down to A J 9 7 of trumps. When she ruffs with the 7 I overruff with the queen and exit with a diamond. East has to ruff and concede the last trick to the king of hearts. The full hand was:

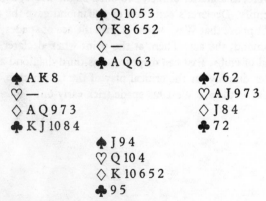

♠ Q 10 5 3
♡ K 8 6 5 2
◇ —
♣ A Q 6 3

♠ A K 8
♡ —
◇ A Q 9 7 3
♣ K J 10 8 4

♠ 7 6 2
♡ A J 9 7 3
◇ J 8 4
♣ 7 2

♠ J 9 4
♡ Q 10 4
◇ K 10 6 5 2
♣ 9 5

"If it had been anyone else playing it, I would have doubled three hearts," said the lady in the East chair politely.

"Then you might have put in a higher heart on the first round," commented her husband.

Post-mortem

This was the situation round the table at the point shown in the diagram:

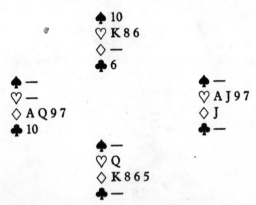

                    ♠ 10
                    ♡ K 8 6
                    ◇ —
                    ♣ 6

    ♠ —   ♠ —
    ♡ —   ♡ A J 9 7
    ◇ A Q 9 7   ◇ J
    ♣ 10   ♣ —

                    ♠ —
                    ♡ Q
                    ◇ K 8 6 5
                    ♣ —

The sequence was: diamond ruff, club ruffed by the queen, diamond ruffed by East, who had to give the last trick to the king of hearts.

West was right in suggesting that the 7 of hearts from East at trick three would have altered the development of the play, but I don't think East can be seriously blamed.

There were, as a matter of fact, two other slight errors, by no means easy to identify. Declarer's early ruff of a diamond gave the defenders a chance. Suppose that West, when in with the ace of spades, had led a second diamond, the ace. Then, at the point when declarer leads the third round of clubs, East can dispose of his third diamond and South cannot enter dummy for the critical play of the fourth club. The best order of play is to give West his spade trick early on.

136

42. Scissors Movement

In a multiple team event both sides are vulnerable and I hold as dealer:

$$\spadesuit \text{A K J 5} \quad \heartsuit \text{8} \quad \diamondsuit \text{J 8 5} \quad \clubsuit \text{K 10 9 7 2}$$

I open **one club,** my partner responds **one heart,** and East, on my right, comes in with **three diamonds.** Annoying, but a double would be too risky and I can hardly bid three spades, so I pass. However, partner is there with a leap to **five clubs.** This is passed out, so the bidding has been:

South	West	North	East
1♣	pass	1♡	3◇
pass	pass	5♣	pass
pass	pass		

West leads the 10 of diamonds and North puts down what in my club we call a "Marilyn Monroe" (i.e. shapely):

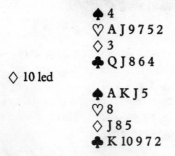

```
              ♠ 4
              ♡ A J 9 7 5 2
              ◇ 3
              ♣ Q J 8 6 4
◇ 10 led
              ♠ A K J 5
              ♡ 8
              ◇ J 8 5
              ♣ K 10 9 7 2
```

East takes the first trick with the queen of diamonds and studies the situation for a while. I dare say he is thinking of playing a second diamond to shorten the dummy. If he does that I will probably be able to cross-ruff for eleven tricks. But in the end he plays ace and another club, West discarding a spade.

I have only three trumps in dummy now for four possible losers, but there must be a good chance to get the hearts going. When I lead a heart, however, West puts in the queen, and on the next round East

137

discards. After a diamond ruff and another heart ruff I arrive at this position:

```
        ♠ 4
        ♡ J 9 7
        ◇ —
        ♣ Q J

        ♠ A K J 5
        ♡ —
        ◇ J
        ♣ 10
```

West still holds K x of hearts, so I cannot establish the long heart. As West discarded a spade at his first opportunity he probably began with five. In that case he will have responsibilities to carry in spades as well as hearts. What is he going to throw if I lead another diamond? A spade, no doubt, and so he does. Now the spades should drop; I play ace, king and another, and the jack of spades wins the last trick, the full hand being:

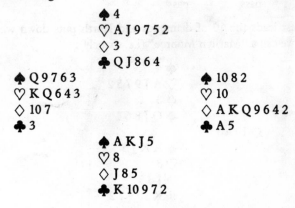

```
              ♠ 4
              ♡ A J 9 7 5 2
              ◇ 3
              ♣ Q J 8 6 4

♠ Q 9 7 6 3                    ♠ 10 8 2
♡ K Q 6 4 3                    ♡ 10
◇ 10 7                         ◇ A K Q 9 6 4 2
♣ 3                            ♣ A 5

              ♠ A K J 5
              ♡ 8
              ◇ J 8 5
              ♣ K 10 9 7 2
```

Post-mortem

This was not a difficult contract to make, admittedly. The reader may think that declarer had only to "play cards." However, a player who did not appreciate the squeeze possibilities might have taken the spade finesse, or tried to ruff out the queen, instead of playing the third round of diamonds.

Sometimes it is not at all easy to see that a defender can be caught in this type of scissors movement. There was a well-known hand in the 1970 Pairs Olympiad:

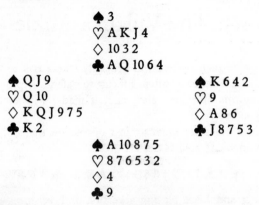

```
              ♠ 3
              ♡ A K J 4
              ◇ 10 3 2
              ♣ A Q 10 6 4
♠ Q J 9                        ♠ K 6 4 2
♡ Q 10                         ♡ 9
◇ K Q J 9 7 5                  ◇ A 8 6
♣ K 2                          ♣ J 8 7 5 3
              ♠ A 10 8 7 5
              ♡ 8 7 6 5 3 2
              ◇ 4
              ♣ 9
```

West was the dealer and usually opened one diamond. Some North – South pairs, having observed that the computer-dealt hands in this tournament seemed to favour distributional slams, propelled themselves into six hearts after a competitive auction.

The defence began with two rounds of diamonds, South ruffing. Two rounds of trumps were drawn, East discarding a diamond. Now if declarer starts a cross-ruff he cannot get a long card going in either black suit; only two spade ruffs are available, and though the club finesse wins, the suit is 5 – 2.

But observe the effect of ruffing the third diamond: whichever suit East discards, declarer has enough entries to establish an extra trick.

43. The Villain's Ankle

In a pairs event good players will generally take a risk to play in six notrumps. This contract is often difficult to defend, it provides scope for various forms of expert play, and, if made, will almost always produce a good score.

Playing in a big pairs event against opposition that does not look unduly formidable, I hold as dealer:

♠ A K J   ♡ J 8 6 3   ◇ A K 7   ♣ A 6 4

My partner and I are playing a version of Precision, with asking bids, so it may be better on this occasion to present the bidding and then explain the conventional calls.

South	West	North	East
1♣	pass	1♠	pass
1NT	pass	2◇	pass
2♠	pass	3♣	pass
3NT	pass	4NT	pass
6NT	pass	pass	pass

One club is conventional and strong; **one spade** is natural and positive; **one notrump** asks for controls and **two diamonds** shows three (counting two for an ace, one for a king). **Two spades** is an asking bid in spades and the response of **three clubs** shows a five-card suit with one of the top honours. The rest of the bidding is natural.

West leads the king of hearts and partner goes down with:

♠ Q 10 9 6 3
♡ A 10
◇ J 6 4
♣ K 9 8

♡ K led

♠ A K J
♡ J 8 6 3
◇ A K 7
♣ A 6 4

Even with this favourable lead there are only eleven tricks in sight. Not surprising, because we have both overbid a little. He might have passed three notrumps and I might have passed four notrumps; but there it is, in this type of event one tends to play for "tops."

For the moment, all I can do is win the heart lead and play off five rounds of spades. On the third round West discards a heart, and on the fourth round East discards ◇ 2 and West ◇ 5. On the last spade both defenders throw a club, West with some reluctance. I have discarded a diamond and a club meanwhile, and these cards are left:

♠ —
♡ 10
◇ J 6 4
♣ K 9 8

♠ —
♡ J 8 6
◇ A K
♣ A 6

Let's do a little reconstruction. West's first discard was a heart, suggesting that he began with K Q 9 x x. As East's first discard was a low diamond and West was unwilling to throw a second diamond, I am inclined to place him with an original Q 10 x x. If so, he is 2 – 5 – 4 – 2 and has discarded one of his two clubs.

I still don't see where the twelfth trick is coming from. The only way to exert any pressure, if my reading of the distribution is correct, is to take two rounds of clubs. West may make the mistake of discarding a second heart. I play off king and ace of clubs, therefore, and West, who followed with the jack on the first round, releases a diamond on the second. All follow to the ace of diamonds. We are now down to:

♠ —
♡ 10
◇ J 6
♣ 9

♠ —
♡ J 8 6
◇ K
♣ —

West has bared the queen of diamonds, I am sure, but on the surface that won't help, as I am cut off from dummy. However, an amusing situation has arisen—amusing to some, anyway. After the king of diamonds has dropped West's queen I lead a low heart. West cannot duck because then the jack of diamonds will win the twelfth trick. He plays the queen and has to lead into my J 8, the full hand being:

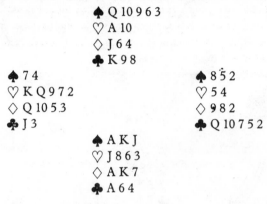

♠ Q 10 9 6 3
♡ A 10
◇ J 6 4
♣ K 9 8

♠ 7 4
♡ K Q 9 7 2
◇ Q 10 5 3
♣ J 3

♠ 8 5 2
♡ 5 4
◇ 9 8 2
♣ Q 10 7 5 2

♠ A K J
♡ J 8 6 3
◇ A K 7
♣ A 6 4

Post-mortem

Could West have discarded better? I don't think so. Observe the position when the second club was led:

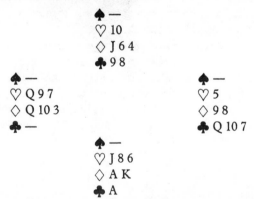

♠ —
♡ 10
◇ J 6 4
♣ 9 8

♠ —
♡ Q 9 7
◇ Q 10 3
♣ —

♠ —
♡ 5
◇ 9 8
♣ Q 10 7

♠ —
♡ J 8 6
◇ A K
♣ A

West was right to discard a diamond—a heart would obviously have been fatal. The dummy, being entryless, should have been dead, but like the stage character who, seemingly eliminated at the beginning of the struggle, survives to grasp the villain's ankle even as he pulls the trigger, North still had a role to play.

44. One That Got Away

Some forms of play, like some politicians and film actresses, get more publicity than others. An opportunity arose on the deal below for a skilful move that has certainly been noted in bridge literature, but so seldom that it will be new to most readers.

Playing rubber bridge in good company, I hold in third position:

♠ 6   ♡ A 6 5 4 2   ◇ 9 6 5 3   ♣ 10 7 4

My partner opens **two notrumps,** I respond **three hearts,** and he give me **four hearts,** completing a brief auction:

South	West	North	East
—	—	2NT	pass
3♡	pass	4♡	pass
pass	pass		

West leads the 9 of hearts and a fairly suitable dummy goes down:

♠ A 9 3
♡ K Q J
◇ K Q J 4
♣ A J 8

♡ 9 led

♠ 6
♡ A 6 5 4 2
◇ 9 6 5 3
♣ 10 7 4

East drops the 10 of hearts on the first trick and fears of a 4 – 1 break are confirmed when he discards the 6 of clubs on the second round. I play off a third heart, East completing an echo in clubs, and then contemplate this situation:

♠ A 9 3
♡ —
◇ K Q J 4
♣ A J 8

♠ 6
♡ A 6
◇ 9 6 5 3
♣ 10 7 4

No one has discarded a spade, unfortunately. If I play the ace of spades and ruff a spade, then draw the last trump, I shall inevitably lose three more spade tricks when the opponents come in with the ace of diamonds.

I must play on diamonds, then, risking a diamond ruff. On the king of diamonds East plays the 7 and West the 8. East wins the next diamond and gives his partner the feared ruff. West switches to the 9 of clubs and East wins with the queen. The omens are bad now. East returns a spade and, sure enough, I have to lose another club at the finish, the full hand being:

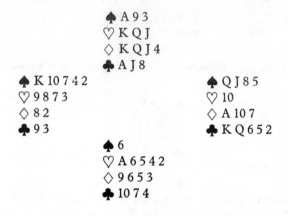

♠ A 9 3
♡ K Q J
◇ K Q J 4
♣ A J 8

♠ K 10 7 4 2
♡ 9 8 7 3
◇ 8 2
♣ 9 3

♠ Q J 8 5
♡ 10
◇ A 10 7
♣ K Q 6 5 2

♠ 6
♡ A 6 5 4 2
◇ 9 6 5 3
♣ 10 7 4

Post-mortem

The hand stayed in my mind, not because I was conscious of having misplayed it, but because it seemed puzzling that I had been unable to arrive at the ten tricks that were there on top. I reconstructed the general position after three rounds of trumps:

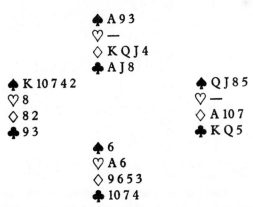

```
            ♠ A 9 3
            ♡ —
            ◇ K Q J 4
            ♣ A J 8
♠ K 10 7 4 2            ♠ Q J 8 5
♡ 8                    ♡ —
◇ 8 2                  ◇ A 10 7
♣ 9 3                  ♣ K Q 5
            ♠ 6
            ♡ A 6
            ◇ 9 6 5 3
            ♣ 10 7 4
```

Eventually a memory stirred and I saw the answer: declarer must exit from dummy with a *low* spade. Say that West wins and leads a club to his partner's queen. East returns a spade; South ruffs, draws the outstanding trump, and forces out the ace of diamonds, with everything under control.

Here is a deal of the same type, where the play is perhaps easier to spot:

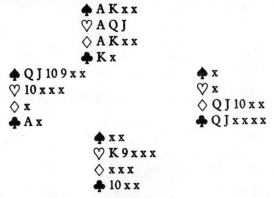

```
            ♠ A K x x
            ♡ A Q J
            ◇ A K x x
            ♣ K x
♠ Q J 10 9 x x          ♠ x
♡ 10 x x x             ♡ x
◇ x                   ◇ Q J 10 x x
♣ A x                 ♣ Q J x x x x
            ♠ x x
            ♡ K 9 x x x
            ◇ x x x
            ♣ 10 x x
```

West opens a weak two spades and South becomes declarer at four hearts. Dummy wins the spade lead and lays down A Q J of hearts. If declarer comes to hand by playing off the king of spades and ruffing a spade he will lose three spades and the ace of clubs, never enjoying a club trick.

As in the original situation, the winning line is to leave the table with a low spade. Say that West wins and leads a diamond. South ruffs the next spade, draws the fourth trump, and leads a club, easily establishing his tenth trick.

45. Call the Director

Two successive hands in a pairs event have proved difficult, and when we come to the last board of the set we are behind the room. As dealer, with neither side vulnerable, I hold:

♠ K J 4   ♡ A Q   ◇ A K Q 6 2   ♣ A Q 10

No problem here: I open **two clubs,** intending to rebid three no-trumps over a negative response. However, partner gives me a positive, **two spades.** It may be important to get in a bid of notrumps from my side, so I mark time with two notrumps. He follows with **three hearts,** I bid **three spades,** and he **three notrumps.** As the last call limits his hand I don't think any grand slam can be a good proposition, so I settle for **six notrumps.** The bidding has been:

South	West	North	East
2♣	pass	2♠	pass
2NT	pass	3♡	pass
3♠	pass	3NT	pass
6NT	pass	pass	pass

West leads the 3 of clubs and partner's hand is about what I expected:

♠ A 10 9 6 3
♡ K 8 4 2
◇ 5
♣ 8 6 2

♣ 3 led

♠ K J 4
♡ A Q
◇ A K Q 6 2
♣ A Q 10

East plays the king of clubs on the first trick and I win with the ace. On the king of spades West discards a diamond, so we are well out of a spade contract. I follow with the jack of spades, West throws a club, and I play low from dummy. When East goes into one of his learned trances

I show him my cards, implying that he can take the queen of spades, but that's all.

If I thought I was saving time, I was wrong. East is not satisfied. My cards are lying on the table now, and looking at them again I realise that I have miscounted the tricks; or rather, have not taken into account that there is an entry problem. Eventually East plays low on the jack of spades, signifying that he wants me to play on. Having made a claim, I have to leave my cards on the table.

There are only eleven tricks on top—three spades, three hearts, three diamonds, and two clubs. I can clear the spades by playing ace and another, but to enter dummy for the fifth spade I will have to overtake the queen of hearts with the king.

However, I am not very worried, because West has thrown a diamond, probably from length. He must be under some pressure already. Come to think of it, what's he going to throw on the next round of spades?

The safest game, no doubt, is to test the diamonds, but if West has length in three suits he will be in bad trouble. I cash the ace and queen of hearts, then the queen of clubs (a *Vienna coup*), on which West drops the 9. The position is:

♠ A 10 9
♡ K 8
◇ 5
♣ 8

♠ 4
♡ —
◇ A K Q 6 2
♣ 10

Although he can see all the cards, West is evidently under great stress when I lead a spade to the ace. He must be down to two hearts, four diamonds, and the jack of clubs. Finally, he lets go the club. After the ace of spades I play the king of hearts, discarding my 10 of clubs, then the 8 of clubs from dummy. Now, with the tournament director urging us to hurry, West surrenders. The progressive squeeze has been worth two tricks, as is apparent from the full diagram:

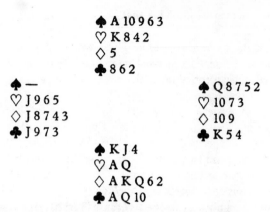

```
              ♠ A 10 9 6 3
              ♡ K 8 4 2
              ◇ 5
              ♣ 8 6 2
♠ —                          ♠ Q 8 7 5 2
♡ J 9 6 5                    ♡ 10 7 3
◇ J 8 7 4 3                  ◇ 10 9
♣ J 9 7 3                    ♣ K 5 4
              ♠ K J 4
              ♡ A Q
              ◇ A K Q 6 2
              ♣ A Q 10
```

"*Thank* you, partner," said West, somewhat bitterly.

I felt a little guilty at making seven, because a player is not supposed to benefit from an incorrect claim. "I think my claim put you off," I said. "Let's score it as six notrumps, just made." And so it was agreed.

Post-mortem

When East saw that I had miscalculated, his best line* would have been to take the queen of spades and return a spade. As the ace and queen of hearts had not been played off, this defence would have left me with only eleven tricks on top. To make the contract, I would have had to negotiate a squeeze against West in the minor suits.

There is no particular moral to the story other than that before making a claim it is advisable to count the certain tricks; and then count them again.

* When an article containing his hand appeared in the American *Bridge World*, the editor appended a footnote: "No, his best line was to summon the tournament director, who would have ruled that the contract was one down." Well, that may be right. The wording of the law about disputed claims is: "The Director determines the result on the board, awarding any doubtful trick to the claimant's opponents."

46. A Little Doze

Our opponents in a team match, like ourselves, are playing the Precision system, in which an opening one diamond is used on a wide variety of hands. I pick up in fourth position:

♠ A Q J   ♡ K Q   ◇ K Q J 9   ♣ Q 10 7 3

We are vulnerable, they are not. After two passes East opens **one diamond** in front of me. I **double,** my partner responds **one heart,** and I jump to **two notrumps,** which about expresses my values. Partner raises to **three notrumps** and all pass.

South	West	North	East
—	pass	pass	1◇
double	pass	1♡	pass
2NT	pass	3NT	pass
pass	pass		

West leads the 4 of clubs and, as expected, there is not much in the dummy:

```
              ♠ 10 4 3
              ♡ A 10 5 2
              ◇ 8 7 4 3
              ♣ 5 2
♣ 4 led
              ♠ A Q J
              ♡ K Q
              ◇ K Q J 9
              ♣ Q 10 7 3
```

East takes the first trick with the king of clubs and continues with ace and another. I win with the queen, discarding a diamond from dummy, and lead the king of diamonds. East wins the second round, to which West follows, and returns a diamond, West discarding the 5 of spades. On a fourth diamond West discards the 2 of spades, dummy a spade, and East, after some consideration, the 3 of hearts. That leaves:

♠ 10 4
♡ A 10 5 2
◇ —
♣ —

♠ A Q J
♡ K Q
◇ —
♣ 10

I have lost three tricks and can afford to lose only one more. I don't quite see how I'm going to do that, though it's easy enough to place the remainder of the cards. West has been at pains to show his partner four spades; East is down to K x x of spades and three hearts, probably headed by the jack. (If he had not held ♡ J, in addition to the other cards with which he is marked, he would have opened a weak notrump.)

Ace and queen of spades will achieve nothing. What about king of hearts, overtake the queen, finesse spade, exit with club? No, West will have a heart to lead to the jack. More by luck than judgement, I dare say, he has discarded well.

I've been a bit slow about this. If I lead the 10 of clubs, what will East discard? In a funny way, he'll be squeezed. West, who was having a little doze, finds himself in possession of an unexpected trick, but East is not enjoying it. He finally lets go a heart. I win the next trick with the king of hearts, and as all the hearts are good when I overtake the queen and the jack falls, I don't even need to finesse in spades. The full hand was:

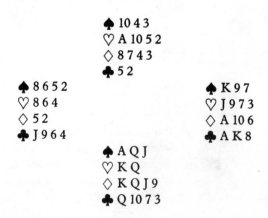

♠ 10 4 3
♡ A 10 5 2
◇ 8 7 4 3
♣ 5 2

♠ 8 6 5 2
♡ 8 6 4
◇ 5 2
♣ J 9 6 4

♠ K 9 7
♡ J 9 7 3
◇ A 10 6
♣ A K 8

♠ A Q J
♡ K Q
◇ K Q J 9
♣ Q 10 7 3

This was the position after the fourth round of diamonds:

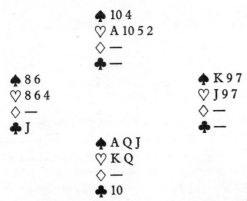

```
              ♠ 10 4
              ♡ A 10 5 2
              ◇ —
              ♣ —
  ♠ 8 6                    ♠ K 9 7
  ♡ 8 6 4                  ♡ J 9 7
  ◇ —                      ◇ —
  ♣ J                      ♣ —
              ♠ A Q J
              ♡ K Q
              ◇ —
              ♣ 10
```

The lead of the 10 of clubs set up a forced suicide squeeze. A spade was thrown from dummy (a heart is also good enough), and obviously East had no good discard.

At the other table the bidding and opening lead were the same, but my team-mates produced a much more dynamic defence. Appreciating that there was no need to continue clubs and that declarer's problem was going to be to obtain enough leads up to his own hand, East made the fine play of a low heart at trick two. When he came in with the ace of diamonds he led a second heart. Forced to play away from his own hand thereafter, South lost three clubs, a diamond and a spade.

47. A Brand from the Burning

Playing in a pairs event with a partner who rarely plays duplicate and whose bidding technique does not extend beyond "strong notrump and Blackwood," I pick up in third position:

♠ A Q 5　♡ A J 10 7 3　◇ K Q 6　♣ A 4

With neither side vulnerable, my partner deals and opens **one club.** I force with **two hearts** and he raises to **three hearts.** To humour him, I bring out the "old Black," **four notrumps.** He responds **five diamonds,** one ace, and I press on with **five notrumps.** Now he bids **six hearts,** showing two kings.

I still don't know whether we ought to be in six hearts or six notrumps, or possibly in a grand slam. The trouble is that he bids one club as an advance guard on widely different types of hand. He may be balanced, but if his clubs are something like K J x x x it may be wiser to play in hearts. We are doing quite well so far, so I think I will pass, making sure of a plus score. The bidding, somewhat undistinguished, has been:

South	West	North	East
—	—	1♣	pass
2♡	pass	3♡	pass
4NT	pass	5◇	pass
5NT	pass	6♡	pass
pass	pass		

West leads the queen of clubs and partner puts down:

♠ J 7 4
♡ K Q 5 2
◇ A 8 4
♣ K 7 6

♣ Q led

♠ A Q 5
♡ A J 10 7 3
◇ K Q 6
♣ A 4

Yes, that's what I was afraid of. Most of the North players will open one notrump and play in six notrumps, which is cold. It's my fault; if I had proceeded more slowly with three spades over three hearts he would have bid three notrumps and we would have finished in the right contract.

Now, what can be done? There are virtually no squeeze possibilities. The only legitimate chance of making an overtrick is to find East with a doubleton king of spades; but there would be little joy in that, because the players in six notrumps would also be making seven.

If East has ♠ K x by any chance, I don't want to fall short of other pairs who may be in six hearts, so I must try to get a picture of the distribution. I have, as a matter of fact, another plan in mind; it fits in with this to eliminate the side suits.

I win the first trick with the ace of clubs and draw the trumps in two rounds. After three rounds of diamonds I play a club to the king and ruff a club, everyone following suit. We are now down to:

♠ J 7 4
♡ Q 5
◇ —
♣ —

♠ A Q 5
♡ J 10
◇ —
♣ —

What are the chances of East holding a doubleton spade? There is just room for West to be 5 – 2 – 3 – 3, but from the way the clubs have been played I am sure he has at least one left. Also, he has obligingly played high-low in diamonds, suggesting an even number. So if anyone has a doubleton spade it is West, not East. I am going to put my other plan into effect.

After a slightly unethical pause (unethical because on this occasion I do *not* want to catch West napping) I lead the ace of spades.

Better! West is pondering. After some tense moments he drops the king of spades.

The full hand was:

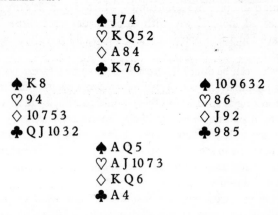

```
                    ♠ J 7 4
                    ♡ K Q 5 2
                    ◇ A 8 4
                    ♣ K 7 6
  ♠ K 8                              ♠ 10 9 6 3 2
  ♡ 9 4                              ♡ 8 6
  ◇ 10 7 5 3                         ◇ J 9 2
  ♣ Q J 10 3 2                       ♣ 9 8 5
                    ♠ A Q 5
                    ♡ A J 10 7 3
                    ◇ K Q 6
                    ♣ A 4
```

Post-mortem

West threw his king of spades under the ace because he placed me with A x x of spades and thought the only chance was to find his partner with Q 10 x x x.

Had West been a first-class player I would not have prepared the mock elimination in such open fashion. It would have been more plausible to lay down the ace of spades early on, this being the normal practice when declarer foresees an elimination ending and does not want to make it easy for a defender with K x or Q x to unblock.

To trap an opponent into making a misguided unblocking play is an art that has not been much developed. Here is another example:

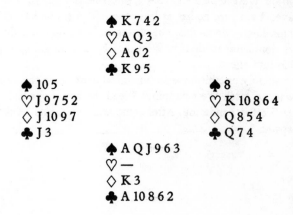

```
                    ♠ K 7 4 2
                    ♡ A Q 3
                    ◇ A 6 2
                    ♣ K 9 5
  ♠ 10 5                             ♠ 8
  ♡ J 9 7 5 2                        ♡ K 10 8 6 4
  ◇ J 10 9 7                         ◇ Q 8 5 4
  ♣ J 3                              ♣ Q 7 4
                    ♠ A Q J 9 6 3
                    ♡ —
                    ◇ K 3
                    ♣ A 10 8 6 2
```

154

North opens a strong notrump and South bids to six spades without mentioning his club suit. West leads the jack of diamonds. South can do better than play off a high club and claim six when no honour falls. He should draw trumps, eliminate the diamonds, then lead a club to the king and return a club. East, placing South with something like ♠ A Q J x x x ♡ x x ◊ K x ♣ A 10 x, may well unblock in clubs to avoid being thrown in and forced to lead a red suit.

48. An Awkward Corner

Some forms of play, like the Cyclops, have no name and belong to no recognised group, yet they help to win innumerable contracts. I am thinking of the type of play—or sequence of plays—that creates uncertainty in an opponent's mind so that, when he gains the lead, he blunders. Style and personality play a large part in this area. Dick Lederer, a giant of the game in the nineteen thirties, with whom I played my first season of "big bridge," had a remarkable instinct for such play. Defending against him, one always seemed to be in an awkward corner. The deal below was just a matter of finding a queen finesse, but it gives an indication of what I have in mind.

Playing rubber bridge against opponents of average strength, I hold in fourth position:

$$\spadesuit A 8 6 \quad \heartsuit J 10 7 5 \quad \diamondsuit K 10 8 2 \quad \clubsuit 7 4$$

Both sides are vulnerable and after a pass by the dealer my partner opens **one diamond**. I respond **one heart** and he raises to **three hearts**. It is seldom a good thing for both players to have length in the same side suit, but I must go to **four hearts** nevertheless. The bidding has been:

South	West	North	East
—	pass	1◇	pass
1♡	pass	3♡	pass
4♡	pass	pass	pass

After some consideration West leads the 2 of hearts and I see that partner was on the low side for his double raise:

♠ Q
♡ Q 9 8 3
◇ A J 7 4
♣ A Q 3 2

♡ 2 led

♠ A 8 6
♡ J 10 7 5
◇ K 10 8 2
♣ 7 4

East plays the king of hearts on the opening lead and returns a heart to his partner's ace. West plays a third round, East discarding a low spade.

These trump leads have left me rather short of tricks. With only one trump left in each hand, I need to find both the club king and the diamond queen. Assuming, as I must, that West has the king of clubs, have I any guide to the position of the diamond queen? A slight indication, perhaps, from the opening lead; West may have led a trump from A x x because he had "difficult" holdings in the other suits.

Anyway, the diamonds can wait. For the moment I lead the 7 of clubs and finesse the queen, which holds. The position is now:

♠ Q
♡ Q
♢ A J 7 4
♣ A 3 2

♠ A 8 6
♡ 10
♢ K 10 8 2
♣ 4

I can ruff only one spade in dummy, so it may be a good idea to lead the queen and duck it. If West has the king he may be uncertain what to play next.

East in fact plays low on the queen of spades and I let it run to West's king. West now goes into a small trance. It is easy to see what is bothering him. He is nervous of leading a club in case I hold J x x. (My lead of the 7 may have played some part in this; East played the 6 on the first round and this may have looked to West like the beginning of an echo from 6 /4.) West is also nervous of returning a spade in case I hold some tenace combination.

Eventually he exits with a low diamond. East puts in the 9 and I win with the 10. Well, I think the diamonds are 3 – 2, but I had better play off a few more cards in case something unexpected turns up. I play ace and another spade, ruffing in dummy, then ace and another club, everybody following. West must surely have at least one diamond left, because with 5 – 3 – 1 – 4 distribution, together with an ace and two kings, he would have taken some action over my one heart, especially as he had passed originally. I play the king of diamonds from hand, therefore, and claim the rest when West follows suit. The full hand was:

                    ♠ Q
                    ♡ Q 9 8 3
                    ◇ A J 7 4
                    ♣ A Q 3 2
♠ K 9 5 2   ♠ J 10 7 4 3
♡ A 4 2   ♡ K 6
◇ 6 5   ◇ Q 9 3
♣ K 10 8 5   ♣ J 9 3
                    ♠ A 8 6
                    ♡ J 10 7 5
                    ◇ K 10 8 2
                    ♣ 7 4

Post-mortem

Whether West's diamond exit was a mistake, or just a wrong guess, is beside the point. The object of declarer's play was to create a situation in which the defence might go wrong.

There are many confusing little plays like the apparent finesse of the queen of spades in the present hand. For example, with A x x x x in dummy opposite a singleton Q in hand, a low card from the table is often worth trying, because a defender with K x x may not put up the king. And there are several variations of the following play:

                    ♡ J x x
                    ◇ J x

                    ♡ A x x
                    ◇ A K x

Playing in a spade contract, with a spare trump in dummy, declarer has two likely losers in hearts. The best way to avoid one of them is to lead a low diamond from hand. West, holding ◇ Q, will not place South with the A K and will not necessarily play the queen. More subtle, with J 10 in dummy, A x x in hand, declarer may begin with a low card towards the 10, which will lose to East. Later, he leads low to the jack, and West, with the other high card, may pass it.

49. Pressure on the Nerve

Playing in a Camrose match (the home international series), I hold in third position:

♠ K Q 3 2   ♡ K 6   ◇ K J 7 2   ♣ A K 4

With both sides vulnerable, my partner passes and East, on my right, opens **one heart.** An overcall of one notrump would express my general values, but I have good support for spades, so I **double.** Partner responds two clubs and East passes. I don't like my hand much, despite its 19 points, but I press on with **two notrumps.** Partner raises to **three notrumps,** and there we rest after this bidding:

South	West	North	East
—	—	pass	1♡
double	pass	2♣	pass
2NT	pass	3NT	pass
pass	pass		

West leads the 4 of hearts and I await the dummy with no great confidence.

```
              ♠ A 10 4
              ♡ 9 7 5
              ◇ Q 8 5
              ♣ J 9 6 3
♡ 4 led
              ♠ K Q 3 2
              ♡ K 6
              ◇ K J 7 2
              ♣ A K 4
```

East puts in the jack of hearts on the opening lead and I win with the king. As East probably has at least five hearts and the ace of diamonds, I need to take eight more tricks in a hurry.

If all goes well I may make four tricks in spades and four in clubs. As the jack of spades may be doubleton, I begin with king and ace of spades, on which all play low.

Even if the spades are breaking I shall need to drop the queen of clubs in two rounds, so let's put that to the test. I play off ♣ A K and the queen from East falls on the second round. A finesse of the 9 of clubs wins, East discarding the 10 of diamonds. The position is now:

♠ 10
♡ 9 7
♦ Q 8 5
♣ J

♠ Q 3
♡ 6
♦ K J 7 2
♣ —

On the jack of clubs East discards the 3 of hearts. The only question now is whether he began with three spades and six hearts or, as I have tended to assume, four spades and five hearts. Am I to play off the queen of spades, hoping for a 3 – 3 break, or can I safely force out the ace of diamonds?

West's lead of the 4 of hearts could have been from 10 x x or from a doubleton 4 2. East might well have played the jack of hearts from A Q J 10 x x. However, with ♡ A Q J 10 x x and ace of diamonds he would probably have bid two hearts over two clubs on the second round.

In the end I play a diamond. East takes the ace and it soon appears that he has only three hearts to cash, the full hand being:

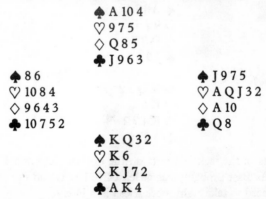

♠ A 10 4
♡ 9 7 5
♦ Q 8 5
♣ J 9 6 3

♠ 8 6
♡ 10 8 4
♦ 9 6 4 3
♣ 10 7 5 2

♠ J 9 7 5
♡ A Q J 3 2
♦ A 10
♣ Q 8

♠ K Q 3 2
♡ K 6
♦ K J 7 2
♣ A K 4

"If I had had Q 10 x of clubs I would also have dropped the queen on the second round," East informed me.

"And I would have been the first to congratulate you," I replied.

Post-mortem

Not a complicated deal, but the order of play was important. First, it was advisable to play off ace and king of clubs before testing the spades. Had West turned up with ♣ Q x, then two more rounds of spades might have been embarrassing for East. When it appeared that East held the doubleton in clubs, it was right to play on clubs. The principle that arises is this: play first the suit which may force the opponent to the greater number of discards.

50. The Best Laid Schemes

There are special hazards in playing on bridgerama, where spectators can follow the play with sight of all four hands. A player must resist the temptation to try any clever play which may look ridiculous if not successful. At the same time he must steel himself to follow what he judges to be the best line.

In the 1960 Olympiad a critical match between Britain and Canada is shown on bridgerama. As dealer, with neither side vulnerable, I hold:

♠ K 10 4   ♡ A 9 4   ◇ Q 8   ♣ K 8 6 5 2

It is common practice nowadays, when playing a weak notrump, to open such hands with one notrump. However, with fair support for both majors and a ragged club suit, I still think **one club** is preferable. Partner forces with **two hearts** and East comes in with **two spades**. With my minimum opening I pass and West raises defensively to **four spades**. Partner bids **five clubs,** and there we play, after this bidding:

South	West	North	East
1♣	pass	2♡	2♠
pass	4♠	5♣	pass
pass	pass		

West leads the 3 of spades and a useful dummy goes down:

♠ 6
♡ K J 10 6 3
◇ A 7 4
♣ A Q J 4

♠ 3 led

♠ K 10 4
♡ A 9 4
◇ Q 8
♣ K 8 6 5 2

East wins the first trick with the ace of spades and returns the 6 of diamonds. I try the queen, but West covers and dummy wins. When I lead the queen of clubs, East discards a spade.

I was expecting the contract to depend simply on the heart finesse, but now I must give the situation a closer look.

♠ —
♡ K J 10 6 3
◇ 7 4
♣ A J 4

♠ K 10
♡ A 9 4
◇ 8
♣ K 8 6 5

If the hearts are 3 – 2 it will be sufficient to finesse the right way, but West's jump to four spades must include a shortage in hearts. Suppose I assume that East has Q x x x. In that case I can play the suit only once before drawing trumps, and meanwhile I have to take care of the spade loser. The first step must be to establish an entry to hand by giving up a diamond.

West takes the diamond trick and plays a third round, which I ruff. The 10 of spades is ruffed and the A J of clubs is cashed. The position is then:

♠ —
♡ K J 10 6 3
◇ —
♣ —

♠ K
♡ A 9 4
◇ —
♣ K

West still has a trump left, so it is impractical to make the normal safety play of laying down the king of hearts. A finesse of the 9 of hearts loses to the queen and West forces my last trump with a diamond. I make the king of spades and lose the last two tricks to a trump and a diamond. The queen of hearts was single, of course, the full hand being:

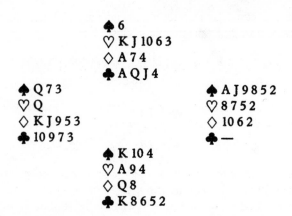

♠ 6
♥ K J 10 6 3
♦ A 7 4
♣ A Q J 4

♠ Q 7 3
♥ Q
♦ K J 9 5 3
♣ 10 9 7 3

♠ A J 9 8 5 2
♥ 8 7 5 2
♦ 10 6 2
♣ —

♠ K 10 4
♥ A 9 4
♦ Q 8
♣ K 8 6 5 2

My partner understood my problems and forbore to comment. But I knew what they would be saying outside: "Six clubs was cold, but Reese went two down in five."

Post-mortem

One critic made the point that, while there were good grounds for placing West with a singleton heart, the singleton was likely to be the queen, as otherwise he might have led it. I don't think there's much in that; with four trumps and a trick in diamonds, he would have led his partner's suit in any case.

Having examined my conscience in the matter, I cannot see that my line of play was wrong. If East's hearts had been Q x x x instead of x x x x I would have made the contract. Because of the entry situation, the finesse in hearts had to be taken on the first round.

51. Double Guard

My partner in a rubber bridge game knows the moves but is not especially bright. I hold in second position:

♠ J 10 2   ♡ J   ◇ A K 10 8 5 3   ♣ A Q 5

There is no score below the line and the opponent on my right opens **one heart.** My hand is not too strong for an overcall of two diamonds, but as it could also play well in spades I decide to **double.** West, on my left, bids **two hearts,** my partner **doubles,** and East passes.

In tournament play the double of two hearts would be regarded as "responsive," putting the ball back in my court. Whether my partner means his double now to be for penalties or responsive, I am not sure. (One of the hazards of playing rubber bridge in a very mixed school is that one never knows whether the weaker players have picked up some point of theory and are assuming that you know that they know, etc.) For the present, I follow the safer course and take out into **three diamonds.** Partner raises to **four diamonds.** Well, I have a six-card suit, I will bid the game, **five diamonds.**

South	West	North	East
—	—	—	1♡
double	2♡	double	pass
3◇	pass	4◇	pass
5◇	pass	pass	pass

West leads the 2 of hearts and partner puts down:

```
            ♠ A 7 5
            ♡ 10 9 7 4
            ◇ Q 6 2
            ♣ K 8 3

    ♡ 2 led

            ♠ J 10 2
            ♡ J
            ◇ A K 10 8 5 3
            ♣ A Q 5
```

Over my three diamonds he might have bid three notrumps, which
I would have been happy to pass. Five diamonds is not going to be
easy.

East wins the heart lead with the king and returns the jack of clubs,
which I take with the ace. On the ace of diamonds West drops the jack.

How am I going to avoid losing two spade tricks? It is not very likely
that either opponent has a doubleton honour. Perhaps I can do something with the hearts. If West began with Q 8 2, for example, I can
make a heart trick by discarding a loser on the 10 of hearts and then
leading the 9, to pin the 8.

I play the king of diamonds and a diamond to the queen, West
discarding two clubs. When I lead the 10 of hearts from dummy East
gives it a brief look, then goes up with the ace. I ruff and play the queen
of clubs, on which East drops the 10. The position is now:

```
            ♠ A 7 5
            ♡ 9 7
            ◇ —
            ♣ K

            ♠ J 10 2
            ♡ —
            ◇ 10 8
            ♣ 5
```

Nobody has thrown a spade and it's impossible for either player to
hold a doubleton Q x or K x. What's the heart situation? With
A K x x x East wouldn't have played the ace on the second round,
making it easy for me to ruff out his partner's queen. He may have false-
carded from A K Q x. If West has 8 x now and East Q x, we have the

elements of a double trump squeeze, because both opponents will be involved in guarding both major suits.

On the 10 of diamonds West discards his fifth club, dummy a spade and East a spade. When I follow with a club to the king West throws a spade and so does East. Obviously they are both keeping two hearts and the remaining spades are 2 – 2. I play off ace and another spade, dropping the jack and 10 from hand, quite unnecessarily! Then I win the last two tricks with a diamond and a spade, the full hand being:

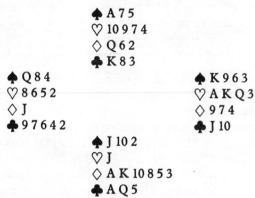

It is rather odd that, with no mistake by the defence, the thirteenth trick should have been won by the 2 of spades.

Post-mortem

This was the position round the table when declarer led a club to the king:

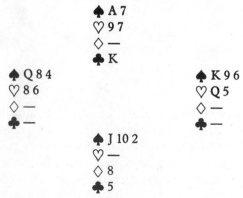

Neither defender could afford to let go a heart, so both discarded a spade.

In the 1948 edition of *Reese on Play* I included the double trump squeeze among a group described as "too rare and difficult of comprehension to be of practical importance." Which shows we have advanced since then, for really the play is not difficult. The distinguishing mark is a combination in dummy (the 9 7 of hearts in this instance) of which declarer is void and which both opponents must guard. Dummy will have the top card in another suit (spades), where the declarer has a possible long card. The squeeze is set in motion by the last trump but one, and at this point there must be two entry cards to the table. The present hand was a "double trump squeeze without the count," inasmuch as a spade trick was lost after the squeeze had begun.

52. Roman Holiday

My opponents in a team-of-four match are playing the Roman system, made famous by the Italian pair, Belladonna and Avarelli. Both sides are vulnerable and in second position I hold:

♠ J ♡ A K Q J 9 2 ◇ K ♣ A J 10 7 4

The opponent on my right opens **two spades.** In the Roman system this signifies a hand in the 12 – 16 range containing at least five spades and at least four clubs. My prospects in a heart contract look quite good, especially if I am going to get a club lead, so having advised the table that I propose to make a "skip" bid, I venture **four hearts.** (The object of the warning is to require the next player to pause for ten seconds before making his call, whatever he may hold; this is supposed to reduce ethical problems arising from slow or quick passes over a pre-empt.) West, after the appropriate interval, **doubles,** and all pass. The bidding has been:

South	West	North	East
—	—	—	2♠
4♡	double	pass	pass
pass			

West leads the 10 of spades and my partner puts down:

```
              ♠ K 9 8 6 5 4
              ♡ 7 6 4
              ◇ 10 9
              ♣ 8 3

♠ 10 led
              ♠ J
              ♡ A K Q J 9 2
              ◇ K
              ♣ A J 10 7 4
```

There is not much in the dummy, but one or two features that may prove helpful. I play low on the spade lead and East wins with the queen. Clearly the lead is a singleton and East gives some thought to returning a spade. A low spade would not be a good defence, as I would discard my losing diamond. East finally decides on a trump, which I take with the ace.

East is marked with at least four clubs by his opening bid, and it looks as though his values consist of the A Q of spades and the K Q of clubs. The ace of diamonds is the only card that West can hold to justify his double of four hearts.

My first idea is to exit with the jack of clubs. East will win and probably play a second round of trumps if he holds one. In that case I can enter dummy with a trump and finesse the 10 of clubs; alternatively, I can cash the ace of clubs and obtain a ruff on the table even if the trumps are 3 – 1.

However, that won't give me the contract. I shall be losing a spade, a diamond, and two clubs. Is there any way of improving on this?

Dummy's spades exert some sort of threat. As the 10, jack and queen went on the first trick, dummy holds K 9 8 6 5 against East's A 7 x x. Unfortunately, there is at most one entry to the table. Still, it means that if trumps are drawn, and they are 2 – 2, the defenders cannot play spades safely; nor can they return a club into the A 10, for then one ruff will establish the suit for me. But of course they can exit with a diamond.

Wait a moment, though! If the trumps are 2 – 2 East will have room for only two diamonds. Suppose I am able to extract those before exiting with a club?

I mustn't play the king of diamonds at once because then West would exit with a trump. I play off a second heart and am pleased to see that all follow. Then I lead the king of diamonds.

West wins and cannot safely exit with a club because then I would want only one club ruff. He plays a second diamond, which I ruff. As planned, I exit with the jack of clubs, East winning with the king. The position is now:

♠ K 9 8 6 5
♡ 7
♢ —
♣ 8

♠ —
♡ Q J 2
♢ —
♣ A 10 7 4

East has only spades and clubs left, and as a spade would enable me to set up several winners he tries a low club. Well, that king of clubs deceived no one. I finesse the 10, ruff a club, and the rest of my hand is high. Somewhat unexpectedly, I have made the contract. This was the full hand:

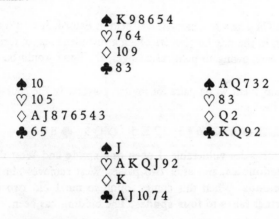

```
              ♠ K 9 8 6 5 4
              ♡ 7 6 4
              ◇ 10 9
              ♣ 8 3
♠ 10                          ♠ A Q 7 3 2
♡ 10 5                        ♡ 8 3
◇ A J 8 7 6 5 4 3             ◇ Q 2
♣ 6 5                         ♣ K Q 9 2
              ♠ J
              ♡ A K Q J 9 2
              ◇ K
              ♣ A J 10 7 4
```

Post-mortem

The precise nature of the opening bid recoiled on the opposition. East was marked at once with five spades and, probably, four clubs. Moreover, West's double placed him with the ace of diamonds, so declarer could be sure that East held both club honours.

The critical moment in the play was when South realised that if he could exhaust East of diamonds he might force a favourable lead in one of the black suits. The lead of the king of diamonds was a rather difficult example of the communication play known as the *Scissors coup*. Of course, it was lucky to find the hearts 2 – 2. Had they been 3 – 1, playing a second round would probably have cost a trick, as the defence would have been able to play a third round before declarer had ruffed a club.

53. Star Part

Early in 1974 a new tournament was held in Estoril. It would not have been easy, in the fine hotel overlooking a turbulent sea, to foresee that within a year, owing to political changes, the hotel would be desolate and empty.

The main event was a pairs for invited players. In the course of this I hold as dealer:

♠ A K 8 6 4 3   ♡ K 5   ◇ Q 3   ♣ 8 6 2

With both sides vulnerable, I open **one spade** and West **doubles**. Partner **redoubles,** and after two passes West removes himself into **two diamonds**. When this comes round to me I bid **two spades**, which partner raises to **four spades**. The bidding has been:

South	West	North	East
1♠	double	redouble	pass
pass	2◇	pass	pass
2♠	pass	4♠	pass
pass	pass		

West leads the king of diamonds and this dummy goes down:

♠ 9 2
♡ A Q 6 4 3
◇ 10 4
♣ A K J 5

◇ K led

♠ A K 8 6 4 3
♡ K 5
◇ Q 3
♣ 8 6 2

North's pass over two diamonds, following his redouble, was forcing; he was giving me a chance to double.

Against four spades West begins with two top diamonds, on which his partner plays high-low, presumably to indicate an even number. After some thought West switches to the 10 of clubs. The finesse is probably right, but I don't need to take it now. I go up with the king and play a spade to the ace, on which the queen appears from West.

As West doubled one spade and cannot have much in high cards, this queen looks very much like a singleton. If so, I shall need to shorten my trumps twice to end up with K 8 x over East's J 10 x. The difficulty about this is that East still holds two diamonds and is not going to follow suit all the time when I play hearts and clubs.

But perhaps that won't matter. I haven't worked out the end-game, but I have an idea that the 9 of spades will come into it.

Clearly the way to begin is king and ace of hearts, followed by the ruff of a low heart. At this point East discards a club. No matter, if his distribution is 4 – 2 – 4 – 3 he will follow to the next club. I shall need master cards in dummy, so I finesse the jack of clubs successfully, arriving at this position:

♠ 9
♡ Q 6
◇ —
♣ A 5

♠ K 8 6 4
♡ —
◇ —
♣ 8

I lead the queen of hearts from dummy. East, I fancy, is down to J 10 7 of spades and two diamonds. He works out that it won't help to ruff with the 10, as I will simply overruff and lead a spade to the 9, just losing to the jack. East discards a diamond, therefore, and I dispose of my last club. When East discards again on the ace of clubs I ruff and exit with a low spade to dummy's 9. East wins and has to return a spade into my K 8, the full hand being:

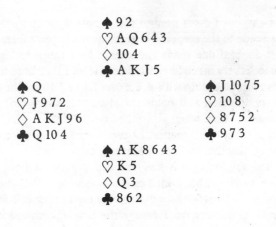

Post-mortem

The sequence of play was two diamonds, club to the king, ace of spades, three rounds of hearts, club to the jack, producing this position:

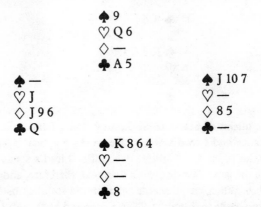

On the queen of hearts East discarded a diamond and South a club. Then the ace of clubs was ruffed and a spade to the 9 left East on play.

Some declarers spoiled their chance by leading a second round of spades from dummy, killing off the star performer (the 9 of spades) too soon. South remains with 8 6 4 3 over East's J 7, but cannot shorten himself twice and be in dummy at trick twelve.

The importance of the 9 of spades is that it relieves declarer of the necessity to cross to dummy after he has taken his two ruffs. In hand at the finish with ♠ K 8 6, he can play low towards dummy's ♠ 9.

54. A New Look

Sometimes one comes across an unusual form of play and thinks, "The chance for that sort of play must occur quite often."

Playing in a strong game of rubber bridge, I hold in third position:

♠ Q 6   ♡ 10 5   ◇ K Q 6   ♣ K 10 9 8 6 2

It is game all and my partner opens **one spade.** I respond **two clubs** and he rebids **two hearts.** I have a fairly close choice now between two spades and two notrumps. As half my points are in diamonds, **two notrumps** seems more natural, though the lack of aces may be a handicap in a close game contract. Partner bids **three notrumps,** and there we rest, after this bidding:

South	West	North	East
—	—	1♠	pass
2♣	pass	2♡	pass
2NT	pass	3NT	pass
pass	pass		

West leads the 3 of diamonds. "Not much for you, I'm afraid," remarks my partner, as he puts down:

♠ K J 9 2
♡ A K Q 2
◇ J 4 2
♣ 4 3

◇ 3 led

♠ Q 6
♡ 10 5
◇ K Q 6
♣ K 10 9 8 6 2

Yes; 14 points or no, I would have passed two notrumps on his hand, which is decidedly short of playing tricks.

There are only seven tricks in sight—three hearts, two spades and two diamonds. What are the chances of getting the clubs going?

Suppose the jack of diamonds holds the first trick and I play a club to the 10, losing to the jack or queen. West exits with a diamond, I cross to the ace of hearts and lead another club. No, I don't like it; no chance at all if the diamonds are 4 – 3, as then I shall lose two diamonds, two clubs and the ace of spades.

Perhaps, instead, I can develop one extra trick in spades and one in clubs. I play low from dummy on the diamond lead, East plays the 10 and I win with the king. The queen of spades is won by West, who after some reflection plays ace of diamonds, on which I drop the queen, followed by another diamond to dummy's jack. East follows suit, but does not play high-low. The 9 of diamonds has not been seen, so on the evidence West began with A 9 x x.

The fact that he played off the ace instead of leading a low diamond suggests that he has a certain entry. There is a case for ducking a club, playing him for a singleton ace. But that seems a little exaggerated; finally I play a low club to the king, on which West drops the queen.

That gives me eight tricks and the next question is how to tackle the spades. The advantage of finessing the 9 as against playing for the drop is not great, and I may have chances even if I fail to drop the 10, so I am not inclined to finesse. Just in case the jack of hearts is single, I play a heart to the queen, then lead the king of spades. Surprise, surprise! East shows out, discarding a heart. The situation requires a new look:

$$\spadesuit \text{ J 9}$$
$$\heartsuit \text{ A K 2}$$
$$\diamondsuit \text{ —}$$
$$\clubsuit \text{ 4}$$

$$\spadesuit \text{ —}$$
$$\heartsuit \text{ 10}$$
$$\diamondsuit \text{ —}$$
$$\clubsuit \text{ 10 9 8 6 2}$$

So West began with six spades. I think I see now why he played off ace of diamonds: he didn't want me, after I had discovered the spade situation, to cash winners in hearts and clubs, then put him on play and force a lead into ♠ J 9.

Is there any chance of end-playing him now? Assuming that he began with six spades and four diamonds, there is only one unknown card. It would not help to find West with Q J of clubs alone, because East would take the ace of clubs and exit with a heart. No, there's only one possibility: West's unknown card must be the jack of hearts.

The strange-looking play of the 2 of hearts from dummy turns out successfully. West wins with the jack, cashes the thirteenth diamond, and has to concede the remaining tricks to dummy's J 9 of spades and top hearts. The full hand was:

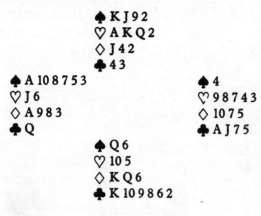

♠ K J 9 2
♡ A K Q 2
◇ J 4 2
♣ 4 3

♠ A 10 8 7 5 3   ♠ 4
♡ J 6   ♡ 9 8 7 4 3
◇ A 9 8 3   ◇ 10 7 5
♣ Q   ♣ A J 7 5

♠ Q 6
♡ 10 5
◇ K Q 6
♣ K 10 9 8 6 2

Post-mortem

This was the situation round the table after East had shown out on the king of spades:

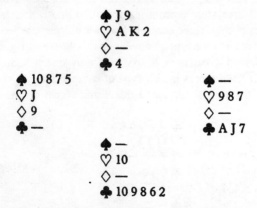

♠ J 9
♡ A K 2
◇ —
♣ 4

♠ 10 8 7 5   ♠ —
♡ J   ♡ 9 8 7
◇ 9   ◇ —
♣ —   ♣ A J 7

♠ —
♡ 10
◇ —
♣ 10 9 8 6 2

One usually plays off the top cards in a suit before exiting; to duck the second heart was certainly unusual, but opportunities for such play cannot be all that rare.

55. A Long Ordeal

In one of the big pairs events at the Europa Hotel I pick up as dealer at love all:

♠ — ♡ A J 9 6 5 ◇ A K J 10 6 2 ♣ A 10

My opponents are two long-haired young persons of indeterminate sex, such as one meets nowadays. Playing Precision, I open a conventional **one club** and the bidding proceeds:

South	West	North	East
1♣	pass	1♠	pass
2♡	pass	3♣	pass
3◇	pass	3NT	pass
4♣	pass	4♠	pass
6♡	pass	pass	pass

In this auction **one spade** was natural and positive; **two hearts** showed a suit and was also an asking bid in hearts; the response of **three clubs** (three steps), promised trump support, at least Q x x, and denied more than three controls (two for an ace, one for a king). The subsequent bids were non-conventional. I knew that a club lead might be awkward if partner's hearts were only queen high, but one has to play for good scores in this type of competition.

West leads the king of clubs and this dummy goes down:

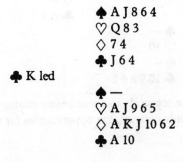

```
        ♠ A J 8 6 4
        ♡ Q 8 3
        ◇ 7 4
        ♣ J 6 4
♣ K led
        ♠ —
        ♡ A J 9 6 5
        ◇ A K J 10 6 2
        ♣ A 10
```

As partner has all the cards he promised, I shall have to take the blame if we don't make it. East plays the 5 of clubs on the first trick, carefully scrutinised by his partner, and I win with the ace.

The best hope must be to enter dummy with a ruff of the third diamond and discard a club on the ace of spades. West drops the queen on the second round and I follow with the 10. West studies this at some length, several times pulling out and replacing a card. Presumably he (or she) has the king of hearts and is wondering (*a*) whether his partner holds the jack of diamonds, and (*b*) whether, if he ruffs, the queen of clubs will stand up. Eventually he discards a club.

Now, what's going on? West certainly noted his partner's 5 of clubs at the first trick. I assumed this was the beginning of an echo to show an even number. If West drew the same conclusion, why didn't he ruff and cash the queen of clubs?

My hunch is that he holds K 10 x x of hearts and expects to make two trump tricks anyway. If that's the case it won't help me to ruff the diamond and discard a club on the ace of spades. I won't be able to control the hand sufficiently to pick up ♡ K 10 x x.

Perhaps another line will work. I discard a club on the 10 of diamonds, cash the ace of hearts to extract East's (presumed) singleton, and lead the jack of diamonds, hoping now that West will ruff. Unfortunately, he does not oblige, and East discards also, which confirms my estimate of the trump division.

When I lead out the remaining diamonds West ponders over each one but continues to hoard his K 10 x of trumps. After the last diamond the situation is:

♠ A J 8
♡ Q 8
♢ —
♣ —

♠ —
♡ J 9 6 5
♢ —
♣ 10

West still holds ♡ K 10 x and two black cards. In a last attempt I ruff the club, return to hand with a spade ruff, and lead a heart to the queen. Exhausted by his long ordeal, West studies this card for a while but finally plays low. I have to lose the last two tricks to the K 10 of hearts, the full hand being:

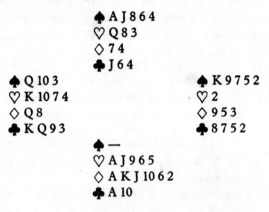

```
                    ♠ A J 8 6 4
                    ♡ Q 8 3
                    ◇ 7 4
                    ♣ J 6 4
    ♠ Q 10 3                       ♠ K 9 7 5 2
    ♡ K 10 7 4                     ♡ 2
    ◇ Q 8                          ◇ 9 5 3
    ♣ K Q 9 3                      ♣ 8 7 5 2
                    ♠ —
                    ♡ A J 9 6 5
                    ◇ A K J 10 6 2
                    ♣ A 10
```

Post-mortem

West may have miscalculated in not ruffing the third diamond with the king of hearts, but thereafter he defended well; if he ruffs a later diamond before disposing of all his spades, I overruff with the 8, discard a club on the ace of spades, and return the queen of hearts, losing just one trump trick.

I thought I'd made a good attempt to land this contract against adverse distribution, but any complacency was soon dispelled.

"You could have made that six hearts, you know", said my partner, half an hour later. "Discard a club on the 10 of diamonds, as you did. Don't cash the ace of hearts, but lead a fourth diamond and ruff with the 3. Then . . ."

"That's no good. East overruffs."

"No, he doesn't. His heart was the 2. You continue with a cross-ruff. At trick 10, when you lead your last diamond, West is down to his four trumps and has to ruff in front of the queen. You still have A J 9 of hearts and you haven't lost a trick."

56. Divide and Rule

My opponents in an international trial are old rivals. We are playing the Butler method of scoring, which is closer to i.m.p. than to match points. With neither side vulnerable I hold in second position:

♠ 10 4   ♡ A Q 6   ◇ K Q J 9 7   ♣ A J 3

The opponent on my right opens **one spade** and I **double**. West, on my left, **redoubles**, and when this comes round to me I take out into **two diamonds**. This is **doubled** by West and now my partner **redoubles**. All such doubles in the part-score area are SOS in our system, so I am being asked to try something else.

This development seems to throw East a little off balance. After confirming that the redouble is a rescue manœuvre, he bids **two hearts**. Evidently he has made a rather weak, distributional opening. I am sure my partner will have something in spades and I am going to risk **two notrumps**. West **doubles** again, concluding an eventful auction:

South	West	North	East
—	—	—	1♠
double	redouble	pass	pass
2◇	double	redouble	2♡
2NT	double	pass	pass
pass			

West leads the 9 of hearts and the dummy is about what I expected:

```
            ♠ J 8 6 5 3
            ♡ 7 4 2
            ◇ 4
            ♣ Q 7 4 2

♡ 9 led
            ♠ 10 4
            ♡ A Q 6
            ◇ K Q J 9 7
            ♣ A J 3
```

East covers the 9 of hearts with the 10, and the first problem is whether or not to hold up. I imagine that East is 5 – 5 in the majors and that West holds the length and high cards in the minors. But West must have more than ace of diamonds and king of clubs for his bidding; no doubt he has an honour in spades as well.

It seems to me that if I take the first heart and play a spade at once I can shut East out of the play. So I take the first trick with the queen of hearts and lead a low spade, on which West plays the king. West leads a second heart and I win with the ace.

The king of diamonds is allowed to hold and I follow with the queen. West takes this and I am happy to note the fall of the 10 from East. West exits with a low club; East plays the 9 and I win with the jack, arriving at this position:

♠ J 8 6
♡ 7
♢ —
♣ Q 7 4

♠ 10
♡ 6
♢ J 9 7
♣ A 3

I have made four tricks and require four more. It is easy enough to find these by way of jack and 9 of diamonds, followed by ace and another club—or followed by the 7 of diamonds, for that matter. But I must have my little joke. After jack of diamonds I tuck away the 9 and lead ace and another club.

West, who was expecting me to cash both diamond winners while in hand, sits up. I let fall a smothered exclamation of dismay. My partner is quite prepared for me to make a foolish error, but he knows my gestures and maintains an even countenance.

On the 3 of clubs West goes up with the king, with the happy vision of giving dummy the lead on the next trick. But now I call for the queen of clubs, and West, after making ♣ 10 8, has to lead into my 9 7 of diamonds at the finish. That gives me eight tricks by way of two hearts, two clubs and four diamonds, the full hand being:

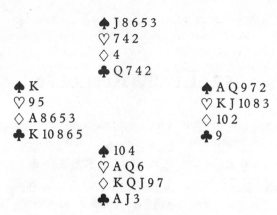

♠ J 8 6 5 3
♥ 7 4 2
♦ 4
♣ Q 7 4 2

♠ K
♥ 9 5
♦ A 8 6 5 3
♣ K 10 8 6 5

♠ A Q 9 7 2
♥ K J 10 8 3
♦ 10 2
♣ 9

♠ 10 4
♥ A Q 6
♦ K Q J 9 7
♣ A J 3

"You bid two notrumps all on your own, with both opponents bidding against you," said West a little ruefully.

"I made eight tricks on my own, too," I pointed out.

Post-mortem

This was the position round the table after the jack of diamonds had been played:

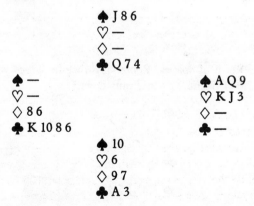

♠ J 8 6
♥ —
♦ —
♣ Q 7 4

♠ —
♥ —
♦ 8 6
♣ K 10 8 6

♠ A Q 9
♥ K J 3
♦ —
♣ —

♠ 10
♥ 6
♦ 9 7
♣ A 3

Almost any sequence of play in the minor suits would win three more tricks, but playing ace and another club (intending to drop the queen under the king) gave West a moment's excitement.

The critical move in the play was the lead of a spade at trick two, effectively shutting East out of the hand. *Divide et impera*, as the Romans used to say.

57. Lively Response

In a not too serious team event I am the dealer with both sides vulnerable. My partner and I are playing Acol and I hold:

♠ K Q J 5 3   ♡ A 10   ◇ A K Q 8 4   ♣ 6

The standards for Acol two bids have risen over the years, but I
consider this hand well worth **two spades.** Partner replies with a
negative **two notrumps** and I follow with **three diamonds.** This
provokes a much more lively response: he jumps to **five clubs,** which
I take to be a cue-bid confirming diamonds. He must have something
more than ace of clubs and diamond support for this leap, so I bid **five
hearts,** admitting to possession of a heart control. He now jumps to
seven diamonds. What have I done?

South	West	North	East
2♠	pass	2NT	pass
3◇	pass	5♣	pass
5♡	pass	7◇	pass
pass	pass		

West leads the 8 of spades. Remarking that he hopes we are not
missing the ace of trumps, partner puts down:

```
              ♠ —
              ♡ K 7 4 3
              ◇ 10 9 6 5 3 2
              ♣ A 9 4
♠ 8 led
              ♠ K Q J 5 3
              ♡ A 10
              ◇ A K Q 8 4
              ♣ 6
```

From his angle, we might indeed have been missing the ace of
diamonds. Over five hearts he could safely have bid five spades, as
obviously diamonds was the agreed suit.

I ruff the spade lead and play a diamond to the ace, as the contract will be lay-down if trumps are 1 – 1. West shows out, however, discarding a heart. Well, I must ruff some more spades until the ace appears; I may even play the whole hand as a cross-ruff.

After ruffing the second spade I play ace of clubs and ruff a club, ruff another spade and another club. On this trick West discards a heart. That's odd! The remaining cards are:

$$\spadesuit\ —$$
$$\heartsuit\ K\,7\,4\,3$$
$$\diamondsuit\ 10\,9$$
$$\clubsuit\ —$$

$$\spadesuit\ Q\,J$$
$$\heartsuit\ A\,10$$
$$\diamondsuit\ K\,Q$$
$$\clubsuit\ —$$

I was about to ruff another spade, but this club discard acts as a sudden brake. East has shown seven clubs and two diamonds and has already followed to three spades. Either he has a fourth spade and is void of hearts, or he has a singleton heart and no more spades. In any case, it won't be safe to cash two hearts, because East will be ruffing.

On all grounds, the hearts are more likely to be 6 – 1 than 7 – 0. But if they *are* 6 – 1, East has no more spades. Could West have underled the ace of spades? Well, we'll soon see. I can draw the outstanding trump and lay down the ace of hearts. If East shows out, spades must be 4 – 4; and if East follows to one round of hearts he can have no more spades.

East does follow to the ace of hearts. Having checked once again, I lead the queen of spades and let it run. West, the dog, has underled the ace of spades, the full hand being:

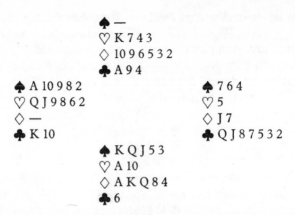

```
                    ♠ —
                    ♡ K 7 4 3
                    ◇ 10 9 6 5 3 2
                    ♣ A 9 4
♠ A 10 9 8 2                        ♠ 7 6 4
♡ Q J 9 8 6 2                       ♡ 5
◇ —                                 ◇ J 7
♣ K 10                              ♣ Q J 8 7 5 3 2
                    ♠ K Q J 5 3
                    ♡ A 10
                    ◇ A K Q 8 4
                    ♣ 6
```

"So that's the sort of game you play," I said to West. "Underleading aces against grand slams."

"What are you talking about?" he replied. "I led fourth best, isn't that right?"

Post-mortem

When I reached the diagram position, there was another way of ensuring the contract. I could have drawn the trump, ruffed a fourth spade, and returned to the ace of hearts. Then, if the ace of spades had not appeared, the last trump would inevitably squeeze West in spades and hearts.

It was, no doubt, fairly clear from the bidding that North had a void in spades. After giving a negative reply he had bid with great vigour to a grand slam, without inquiring for aces. This must signify a void, and the void could only be in the opener's first suit.

Even so, the underlead from the ace was a clever stroke. I certainly began the play in the firm belief that East held the ace of spades and that it would be safe to ruff the suit until the ace had appeared. It was West's bad luck that his shortness in clubs turned up so early and gave me the hint to reassess the position.

58. Below the Waterline

My opponents in a team-of-four match play a studious game. We are vulnerable and in fourth position I hold:

♠ A J 7   ♡ Q 6 4   ◇ K 7 4 2   ♣ K 8 5

West, on my left, opens **one spade** and this is followed by two passes. I reopen with **one notrump,** which we play as 11 – 14 in the protective position, and partner raises to **three notrumps,** which is passed out.

South	West	North	East
—	1♠	pass	pass
1NT	pass	3NT	pass
pass			

West leads the 6 of spades and partner puts down a little of everything:

♠ 6 led

♠ Q 10 2
♡ K J 9 3
◇ Q 6
♣ A 7 6 3

♠ A J 7
♡ Q 6 4
◇ K 7 4 2
♣ K 8 5

It's going to be a close affair. Assuming the hearts go reasonably well, I can see eight tricks and there should be one in the wash.

The first question is where to win the first trick. In a sense, I would like to be in hand to lead up to dummy's hearts, but I am short of entries to do that twice. Instead, I will try the old trick of putting up the queen of spades and dropping the jack from hand. This may possibly encourage West to continue spades when he gains the lead.

East drops the 3 of spades on this trick and when the jack appears West demands to see all the cards again. When the trick has finally been turned I lead the jack of hearts from dummy. This holds, and I follow with a low heart to the queen and ace. West promptly returns a heart.

My small deception in the spade suit has not met with any success. I imagine that East would have played high-low with a doubleton and that West, holding six spades, was able to read the 3 as a singleton.

If West has six spades it must be against the odds for him to hold length in hearts. Despite a feeling the other way, I go up with the king. East shows out, discarding a club.

That's a blow, but if West has ten cards in the majors, other possibilities arise. Could West have a singleton ace of diamonds? No, in that case East's first discard would have been a diamond. More likely, West has A x in diamonds and a singleton club. On a club to the king West drops the jack. I lead a low diamond next, hoping that West will play low and leave himself with the ace alone, but he goes up with the ace and cashes the 10 of hearts. East discards a diamond and I throw a club. The situation now is:

♠ 10 2
♡ —
◇ Q
♣ A 7 6

♠ A 7
♡ —
◇ K 7 4
♣ 8

Time stands still while West considers his next move. He may be thinking of leading the king of spades, to block out my king of diamonds. Eventually he decides to protect his spade trick and plays a diamond to the queen.

I have had plenty of time to think out my next play. I lead the 10 of spades, on which East shows out, and play low from hand. When West, perforce, returns a spade to the ace, East, down to two diamonds and two clubs, is squeezed. The full hand was:

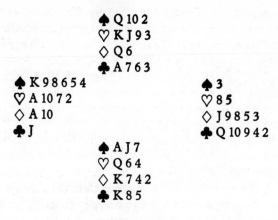

                    ♠ Q 10 2
                    ♡ K J 9 3
                    ◇ Q 6
                    ♣ A 7 6 3
    ♠ K 9 8 6 5 4   ♠ 3
    ♡ A 10 7 2   ♡ 8 5
    ◇ A 10   ◇ J 9 8 5 3
    ♣ J   ♣ Q 10 9 4 2
                    ♠ A J 7
                    ♡ Q 6 4
                    ◇ K 7 4 2
                    ♣ K 8 5

Post-mortem

There were a number of points worth noting in the play: the deceptive manœuvre with the queen and jack of spades; West's conclusion that his partner held a singleton spade, because with 7 3 he would have played high-low; declarer's reading of the distribution; and the combination of submarine and suicide squeeze at the finish.

Suppose that West, after he had cashed the 10 of hearts, had played his alternative defence of leading the king of spades, apparently preventing South from making the queen and king of diamonds separately. Declarer wins with the ace of spades and crosses to dummy's 10. These are the last four cards:

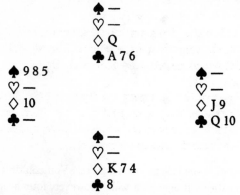

                    ♠ —
                    ♡ —
                    ◇ Q
                    ♣ A 7 6
    ♠ 9 8 5   ♠ —
    ♡ —   ♡ —
    ◇ 10   ◇ J 9
    ♣ —   ♣ Q 10
                    ♠ —
                    ♡ —
                    ◇ K 7 4
                    ♣ 8

South can make three of the last four tricks in a number of ways. Perhaps the prettiest is to cash the queen of diamonds and exit with a *low* club!

59. No Need for Fireworks

At Auction bridge 100 honours was worth almost half the rubber, and I dare say that I have not overcome the habit of respecting them. I can't think of any other explanation for a singularly poor call that I made on the deal that follows.

Third in hand, with neither side vulnerable, I hold:

$$\spadesuit J763 \quad \heartsuit AKQJ9 \quad \diamondsuit Q3 \quad \clubsuit 64$$

Partner opens **one club,** the next player passes, and I respond **one heart.** Partner rebids **one notrump.** Following some train of reasoning that has been obscured by time, I bid **three hearts** instead of the obvious three notrumps, and partner raises to **four hearts,** which is passed out.

South	West	North	East
—	—	1♣	pass
1♡	pass	1NT	pass
3♡	pass	4♡	pass
pass	pass		

West leads the king of clubs and partner puts down:

```
              ♠ A K Q
              ♡ 8 5 3
              ♢ A 10
              ♣ J 9 7 5 2

   ♣ K led

              ♠ J 7 6 3
              ♡ A K Q J 9
              ♢ Q 3
              ♣ 6 4
```

Yes, my rebid of three hearts was a shocker. You couldn't lose three notrumps if you threw it against a wall. However, four hearts doesn't look too difficult.

East plays the 8 of clubs on the first trick and West leads the queen of clubs at trick two. After a moment's consideration East discards the

4 of diamonds. West then leads a low club, East ruffs with the 10 of hearts, and I overruff with the queen. I play off the ace of hearts and the first hint of trouble arises when East discards the 6 of diamonds.

This means that I shall have to play off all the remaining trumps to draw the four held by West. If I do that the spades will be blocked, as there will be no entry back to hand.

One possibility is to play off A K Q of spades before drawing trumps. No, East has already shown up with two singletons. The spades are more likely to be 5 – 1 than 3 – 3.

Let's consider for a moment who has the king of diamonds. Although East has played the 4 and 6, in that order, the 2 is still missing. East would not have signalled for a diamond early on, because he could see the possible advantage of ruffing a club with his singleton trump.

If East has the king of diamonds I can make one of those spectacular plays that turn up more often in books than at the table. I cash two more hearts, on which East discards a spade and a diamond, and a fourth heart, on which I throw the ace of diamonds from dummy. East, with a puzzled frown, discards another diamond. We have arrived at this position:

♠ A K Q
♡ —
♢ 10
♣ J 9

♠ J 7 6 3
♡ —
♢ Q 3
♣ —

After three top spades I lead the 10 of diamonds from the table. East takes the king but has to concede the last two tricks to my jack of spades and queen of diamonds, the full hand being:

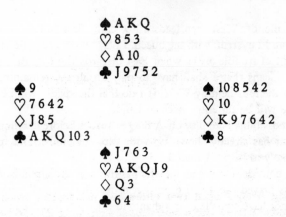

```
              ♠ A K Q
              ♡ 8 5 3
              ◇ A 10
              ♣ J 9 7 5 2
♠ 9                              ♠ 10 8 5 4 2
♡ 7 6 4 2                        ♡ 10
◇ J 8 5                          ◇ K 9 7 6 4 2
♣ A K Q 10 3                     ♣ 8
              ♠ J 7 6 3
              ♡ A K Q J 9
              ◇ Q 3
              ♣ 6 4
```

"Isn't it the same if you keep the A 10 of diamonds in dummy?" asked East, implying that my antics were unnecessary. "When I win with the king of diamonds I have to give you the last spade trick."

Fortunately I was able to answer this. "It depends how you discard," I said. "You can let all your spades go and come down to K x x of diamonds at the finish."

Post-mortem

Has anything struck you about the play of this hand? I wrote it up some years ago as an example of a rare unblocking play. Readers must have been less observant or less critical than they are nowadays, for no one wrote to point out that declarer could succeed by a far simpler line. All he need do is discard a diamond on the third club instead of over-ruffing.

60. The Sea Lawyer

Very slow play by the opposition has caused a team-of-four match to drag on into the early hours. Near the finish, I pick up this handsome collection as dealer:

♠ A K 7   ♡ A Q 2   ◇ K Q J 6   ♣ A K 3

Playing Acol, I open **two clubs** and my partner responds **two diamonds**. I rebid **three notrumps**, suggesting 25 – 26 points. He bids **four clubs**, Baron, asking for my four-card suits upwards. I bid **four diamonds**, he **four spades**, and I **four notrumps**, indicating that I have no more suits to show. He now jumps to **six clubs**.

That is a little unexpected. I imagine he has longer clubs than spades and good values consistent with a negative response. He could hold both black queens and the ace of diamonds. Six notrumps must be safe, so I will test him out with a grand slam try of **six hearts**. After much thought he ventures **seven clubs**, and I transfer to **seven notrumps**. It has been a lengthy auction, both in time and number of bids:

South	West	North	East
2♣	pass	2◇	pass
3NT	pass	4♣	pass
4◇	pass	4♠	pass
4NT	pass	6♣	pass
6♡	pass	7♣	pass
7NT	pass	pass	pass

West leads the 10 of diamonds and I await the dummy with some anxiety. This is what I see:

```
              ♠ Q 9 4 3
              ♡ 6 3
              ◇ A 5
              ♣ Q 10 8 7 5
  ◇ 10 led
              ♠ A K 7
              ♡ A Q 2
              ◇ K Q J 6
              ♣ A K 3
```

Quite well bid by us!

I take the first diamond in dummy and lead a low club, on which East discards a heart.

After a brief calculation, during which the opponents show signs of impatience, I put my cards back in the board. "You don't want me to play this, do you?" I ask.

"Well, let's see what you've got," said West.

I took my cards out again and showed them.

"I can only count twelve tricks," said East, "counting the club finesse."

"There may be only twelve on top," I said, "but it's getting late and . . ."

"Kindly state your line of play," said East firmly.

"Oh, very well. I take two top clubs and three top spades. No problem if the spades break 3 – 3. If West has the long spades, in addition to his five clubs, I cash my red suit winners and squeeze him in the black suits. You agree with that?"

"Yes."

"Suppose, as is more likely, that East has the long spades. I begin as before, then play off two more diamonds, arriving at this position:

♠ 9
♥ 6
♦ —
♣ Q 10 8

♠ —
♥ A Q 2
♦ J
♣ 3

"When I play the last diamond West must keep three clubs, so cannot keep more than one heart. I discard a club from dummy, then follow with two more club winners. This squeezes East, who has control of spades and hearts. I am supposing the full hand to be like this:"

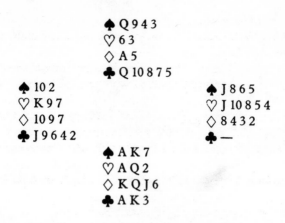

Post-mortem

In the hand as constructed above, the end situation is:

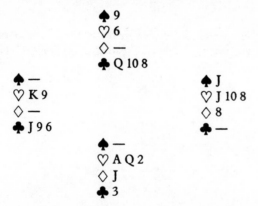

The jack of diamonds forces West to bare the king of hearts, and two rounds of clubs then strangle East.

I asked some questions around this hand once in an *Observer* competition, one of them being, "At what point can South claim the contract?" My answer was, "As soon as East shows out on the first club." One sea lawyer wrote in to dispute this. "East may have revoked," he said. "You cannot claim the contract until the revoke has been established. If East corrects his revoke in time, and if in fact he holds J 9 x x of clubs, the hand is not over."

Ah well, you can't win them all.

THE BEST OF DEVYN PRESS
Newly Published Bridge Books

Bridge Conventions Complete
by Amalya Kearse
$17.95

An undated and expanded edition (over 800 pages) of the reference book no duplicate player can afford to be without. The reviews say it all:

"At last! A book with both use and appeal for expert or novice plus everybody in between. Every partnership will find material they will wish to add to their present system. Not only are all the conventions in use anywhere today clearly and aptly described, but Kearse criticizes various treatments regarding potential flaws and how they can be circumvented.

"Do yourself a favor and add this book to your shelf even if you don't enjoy most bridge books. This book is a treat as well as a classic."
—ACBL BULLETIN

"A must for duplicate fans, this is a comprehensive, well-written guide through the maze of systems and conventions. This should be particularly useful to those who don't want to be taken off guard by an unfamiliar convention, because previously it would have been necessary to amass several references to obtain all the information presented."
—BRIDGE WORLD MAGAZINE
Published January, 1984

Recommended for: all duplicate players

ISBN 0-910791-07-4 paperback

Test Your Play As Declarer, Volume 1
by Jeff Rubens and Paul Lukacs
$5.95

Any reader who studies this book carefully will certainly become much more adept at playing out a hand. There are 89 hands here, each emphasizing a particular point in declarer play. The solution to each problem explains how and why a declarer should handle his hands in a certain way. A reprint of the original.
Published December, 1983

Recommended for: intermediate through expert

ISBN 0-910791-12-0 paperback

Devyn Press Book of Partnership Understandings
by Mike Lawrence
$2.95

Stop bidding misunderstandings before they occur with this valuable guide. It covers all the significant points you should discuss with your partner, whether you are forming a new partnership or you have played together for years.
Published December, 1983

Recommended for: novice through expert

ISBN 0-910791-08-2 paperback

101 Bridge Maxims
by H. W. Kelsey
$7.95

The experience of a master player and writer condensed into 101 easy-to-understand adages. Each hand will help you remember these essential rules during the heat of battle.
Published December, 1983

Recommended for: bright beginner through advanced.

ISBN 0-910791-10-4 paperback

Play Bridge with Mike Lawrence
by Mike Lawrence
$9.95

Follow Mike through a 2-session matchpoint event at a regional tournament, and learn how to gather information from the auction, the play of the cards and the atmosphere at the table. When to go against the field, compete, make close doubles, and more.
Published December, 1983

Recommended for: bright beginner through expert.

ISBN 0-910791-09-0 paperback

Play These Hands With Me
by Terence Reese
$7.95

Studies 60 hands in minute detail. How to analyze your position and sum up information you have available, with a post-mortem reviewing main points.
Published December, 1983

Recommended for: intermediate through expert.

ISBN 0-910791-11-2 paperback

THE BEST OF DEVYN PRESS
Bridge Books

A collection of the world's premier bridge authors have produced, for your enjoyment, this wide and impressive selection of books.

MATCHPOINTS
by Kit Woolsey
$9.95

The long-awaited second book by the author of the classic *Partnership Defense*. *Matchpoints* examines all of the crucial aspects of duplicate bridge. It is surprising, with the wealth of excellent books on bidding and play, how neglected matchpoint strategy has been—Kit has filled that gap forever with the best book ever written on the subject. The chapters include: general concepts, constructive bidding, competitive bidding, defensive bidding and the play.
Published October, 1982
Recommended for: intermediate through expert.
ISBN 0-910791-00-7 paperback

DYNAMIC DEFENSE
by Mike Lawrence
$9.95

One of the top authors of the '80's has produced a superior work in his latest effort. These unique hands offer you an over-the-shoulder look at how a World Champion reasons through the most difficult part of bridge. You will improve your technique as you sit at the table and attempt to find the winning sequence of plays. Each of the 65 problems is thoroughly explained and analyzed in the peerless Lawrence style.
Published October, 1982.
Recommended for: bright beginner through expert.
ISBN 0-910791-01-5 paperback

MODERN IDEAS IN BIDDING
by Dr. George Rosenkranz and Alan Truscott
$9.95

Mexico's top player combines with the bridge editor of the <u>New York Times</u> to produce a winner's guide to bidding theory. Constructive bidding, slams, pre-emptive bidding, competitive problems, overcalls and many other valuable concepts are covered in depth. Increase your accuracy with the proven methods which have won numerous National titles and have been adopted by a diverse group of champions.
Published October, 1982
Recommended for: intermediate through expert.
ISBN 0-910791-02-3 paperback

THE COMPLETE BOOK OF OPENING LEADS
by Easley Blackwood
$12.95

An impressive combination: the most famous name in bridge has compiled the most comprehensive book ever written on opening leads. Almost every situation imaginable is presented with a wealth of examples from world championship play. Learn to turn your wild guesses into intelligent thrusts at the enemy declarer by using all the available information. Chapters include when to lead long suits, dangerous opening leads, leads against slam contracts, doubling for a lead, when to lead partner's suit, and many others.
Published November, 1982.
Recommended for: beginner through advanced.
ISBN 0-910791-05-8 paperback

dp THE BEST OF DEVYN PRESS
Bridge Books

A collection of the world's premier bridge authors have produced, for your enjoyment, this wide and impressive selection of books.

TEST YOUR PLAY AS DECLARER, VOLUME 2
by Jeff Rubens and Paul Lukacs
$5.95

Two celebrated authors have collaborated on 100 challenging and instructive problems which are sure to sharpen your play. Each hand emphasizes a different principle in how declarer should handle his cards. These difficult exercises will enable you to profit from your errors and enjoy learning at the same time.
Published October, 1982.
Recommended for: intermediate through expert.
ISBN 0-910791-03-1 paperback

TABLE TALK
by Jude Goodwin
$5.95

This collection of cartoons is a joy to behold. What Snoopy did for dogs and Garfield did for cats, Sue and her gang does for bridge players. If you want a realistic, humorous view of the clubs and tournaments you attend, this will brighten your day. You'll meet the novices, experts, obnoxious know-it-alls, bridge addicts and other characters who inhabit that fascinating subculture known as the bridge world.
Recommended for: all bridge players.
ISBN 0-910891-04-X paperback

THE CHAMPIONSHIP BRIDGE SERIES

In-depth discussions of the mostly widely used conventions...how to play them, when to use them and how to defend against them. The solution for those costly partnership misunderstandings. Each of these pamphlets is written by one of the world's top experts. **Recommended for: beginner through advanced.**
95 ¢ each, Any 12 for $9.95, All 24 for $17.90

VOLUME I [#1-12]
PUBLISHED 1980

1. Popular Conventions by Randy Baron
2. The Blackwood Convention by Easley Blackwood
3. The Stayman Convention by Paul Soloway
4. Jacoby Transfer Bids by Oswald Jacoby
5. Negative Doubles by Alvin Roth
6. Weak Two Bids by Howard Schenken
7. Defense Against Strong Club Openings by Kathy Wei
8. Killing Their No Trump by Ron Andersen
9. Splinter Bids by Andrew Bernstein
10. Michaels' Cue Bid by Mike Passell
11. The Unusual No Trump by Alvin Roth
12. Opening Leads by Robert Ewen

VOLUME II [#13-24]
PUBLISHED 1981

13. More Popular Conventions by Randy Baron
14. Major Suit Raises by Oswald Jacoby
15. Swiss Team Tactics by Carol & Tom Sanders
16. Match Point Tactics by Ron Andersen
17. Overcalls by Mike Lawrence
18. Balancing by Mike Lawrence
19. The Weak No Trump by Judi Radin
20. One No Trump Forcing by Alan Sontag
21. Flannery by William Flannery
22. Drury by Kerri Shuman
23. Doubles by Bobby Goldman
24. Opening Preempts by Bob Hamman

THE BEST OF DEVYN PRESS ♧

DEVYN PRESS
151 Thierman Lane
Louisville, KY 40207
(502) 895-1354

VISA AND MASTER
CARD ACCEPTED

ORDER FORM

Number
Wanted

_____	101 BRIDGE MAXIMS, Kelsey............................ x $7.95 =	
_____	PLAY BRIDGE WITH MIKE LAWRENCE, Lawrence........x 9.95 =	
_____	PARTNERSHIP UNDERSTANDINGS, Lawrence.......... x 2.95 =	
_____	BRIDGE CONVENTIONS COMPLETE, Kearse.......... x 17.95 =	
_____	PLAY THESE HANDS WITH ME, Reese..................x 7.95 =	
_____	TEST YOUR PLAY AS DECLARER, VOL. 1, Rubens-Lukacs x 5.95 =	
_____	MATCHPOINTS, Woolsey.....................................x 9.95 =	
_____	DYNAMIC DEFENSE, Lawrence ....x 9.95 =	
_____	MODERN IDEAS IN BIDDING, Rosenkranz-Truscott ....x 9.95 =	
_____	COMPLETE BOOK OF OPENING LEADS, Blackwood ....x 12.95 =	
_____	TEST YOUR PLAY AS DECLARER, VOLUME 2, Rubens-Lukacs .x 5.95 =	
_____	TABLE TALK, Goodwin ....x 5.95 =	
_____	PARTNERSHIP DEFENSE, Woolsey ....x 8.95 =	
_____	DEVYN PRESS BOOK OF BRIDGE PUZZLES #1, Sheinwold .....x 4.95 =	
_____	DEVYN PRESS BOOK OF BRIDGE PUZZLES #2, Sheinwold .....x 4.95 =	
_____	DEVYN PRESS BOOK OF BRIDGE PUZZLES #3, Sheinwold .....x 4.95 =	
_____	INDIVIDUAL CHAMPIONSHIP BRIDGE SERIES (Please specify) x .95 =	
_____	TICKETS TO THE DEVIL, Powell ....x 5.95 =	
_____	DO YOU KNOW YOUR PARTNER?, Bernstein-Baron ....x 1.95 =	

SUB TOTAL [_____]

QUANTITY DISCOUNT _ON ABOVE ITEMS:_ _10% over $25, 20% over $50_	_We accept checks, money orders and VISA or MASTER CARD. For charge card orders, send your card number and expiration date._

LESS QUANTITY DISCOUNT [_____]

TOTAL [_____]

_____ THE CHAMPIONSHIP BRIDGE SERIES
VOLUME 1......................................x $9.95 (No further discount) [_____]
_____ THE CHAMPIONSHIP BRIDGE SERIES
VOLUME II ....x 9.95 (No further discount) [_____]
_____ ALL 24 OF THE CHAMPIONSHIP
BRIDGE SERIES ....x 17.90 (No further discount) [_____]

ADD SHIPPING:
60¢ for 1 ITEM
$1.00 FOR 2 ITEMS OR MORE
SHIP TO:

TOTAL FOR BOOKS [_____]
SHIPPING ALLOWANCE [_____]
AMOUNT ENCLOSED [_____]

NAME_____

ADDRESS_____

CITY_____ STATE_____ ZIP _____